Contents

PART I

First-Grade Math

PART II

Second-Grade Math

Foreword

The education of every child is of critical importance to the child's happiness, self-esteem, intellectual vibrancy, and success, whether measured in terms of finances or prestige. In today's high-tech world, mathematics is relevant not only to the goals of education but, more importantly, to the basic survival of each individual in society. Unfortunately, mathematics seems to be the first of the basic curricula in which students lose their natural desire to learn, and it therefore deserves special attention.

We need to remember that children are individuals and that each child develops differently. Those who are blessed with accelerated development—the ability to process information and knowledge more quickly—definitely have an edge because, starting earlier, they have more time to develop and practice sophisticated thinking skills. This does not imply that other children are less capable of learning, just that it takes them a bit longer—and that sometimes they need to take a different route—to get to the same point. Unfortunately, schools usually cannot provide the necessary extra time. But parents *do* have that time—or the motivation to create it.

This book gives parents the opportunity to become true partners in their child's development. Dr. Slavin provides a guide for parents who want to encourage mathematics enrichment and accelerated development in their first- and second-grade children, or to help third-graders who are having some difficulty. He does this in a conversational style that helps parents to decide how to react in all situations, including what to do if things don't go as expected. It suggests good judgment and permits the ultimate flexibility of proceeding at any pace.

An important benefit of this parental involvement is the experience of a meaningful family activity. To be a part of the intellectual growth of one's child is both an obligation and a great joy. This book furnishes the opportunity for parents to help their children to develop their thinking and numeric skills, and have a good time together doing it. That is no small achievement.

You, the parent, are to be congratulated. Your using this book demonstrates that you have an uncommon interest in your child's education. This is just the beginning of a long, wondrous adventure; relax and don't forget to have fun!

Martin Rudolph
Chairman, Math Department
Oceanside High School
Oceanside, New York

Acknowledgments

The person responsible for seeing this project through from start to finish is my editor, Judith McCarthy. Not only did she get me a contract and then very carefully edit the manuscript, but she saw the book wend its way through the entire production process.

Martin Rudolph, Math Chairman at Oceanside High School on Long Island, not only wrote the foreword but actually read through the entire manuscript and greatly strengthened the pedagogy by suggesting subtle changes in how various mathematical concepts were presented.

Diane DeRoy, who has developed math curricula and teaches second-grade math in Woodbury, Connecticut, not only persuaded me to shift two chapters from the first grade to the second grade but made dozens of very useful suggestions that made the book a lot easier to use.

Marcia Samuels, the managing editor, Jude Patterson, the copyeditor, and Colleen Dunlap, who oversaw the book's design, illustration, and typesetting, very competently converted the typed manuscript into a finished book.

I also want to thank my niece, Eleni Zimiles, for patiently going through parts of the manuscript, even though she did put big X's next to some of my answers that happened to be wrong. Eleni, who was in the first grade, thought that the first half of the book was "pretty easy." My niece, Justine, who was three and a half, gave me tips by showing me how she added numbers up to 5 plus 5 by counting on her fingers.

Many of the background materials for this book, as well as some of the best pedagogical ideas, were provided by Lenore Friedman, who has taught math at the elementary, intermediate, and high school levels in the New York City public schools since 1970. And Marilyn Sochalski helped me obtain many state mathematics curricula.

I also want to thank my typist, Hazel Staloff, who was able to turn a partially handwritten manuscript full of numbers into the book you are reading. I want to thank my father, Jack Slavin, who taught math for over 40 years at Madison, Lincoln, Brooklyn Tech, and several other New York City high schools. If all the teachers today could teach math the way my father did, books like this one would not be necessary.

Introduction

Is your child learning all the necessary math at school? Many teachers assign little or no homework in the early grades, and since most schools don't use textbooks for grades one and two, how can you be sure your child is learning the fundamentals? What you need is a short, easy-to-understand book that helps you ensure that your child is mastering the basics and that shows you how to help if the child hits a trouble spot. *Math Foundations for Your First- and Second-Grader* is that book.

Its purpose is to help you help your child to learn math. It tells you exactly what concepts and problems your child must master in the first and second grades. And it provides dozens of helpful techniques that can be used to get your child through any rough spots.

You can use this book for four main purposes. Its primary use is to monitor your child's progress and to make certain that your child is learning all the necessary math skills for the crucial early grades.

Second, this book will help if you already know your child is struggling with math. The minilessons here give you the tools to help your child overcome early difficulties.

Third, *Math Foundations for Your First- and Second-Grader* can also help if your child has been promoted to higher grades—or even to middle school or high school—without having learned basic arithmetic. Sadly, there are many older students who have trouble with higher math only because they are weak in the basics. Nearly all of these students *can* learn higher math, but to do so they must first master the fundamentals. By going through this book and working out all the problems, these students can be brought up to standard in just three or four months.

The fourth use is for home schoolers. There is a large and growing number of children who do not attend school at all but are taught by their parents at home. If you have decided to educate your child this way, you will find this book extremely useful, since all the math covered in the first two grades is included here.

I wrote this book because I have seen a steady decline in the math skills of the college students I teach. Many are unable to learn advanced math and economics concepts simply because they never mastered the basic math they should have learned in the first few grades of school. Other professors from around the country also tell me that many of their students have trouble in their classes because they can't do fifth- and sixth-grade math. And now even the Ivy League colleges have been forced to introduce remedial math courses.

These college students would have had much more success in higher math if they had obtained a solid foundation in math early on. Yet schools are clearly not providing this foundation on their own. It is often difficult for a teacher to give individual attention when classes have as many as 30 students.

The key to improving your child's education is much greater *parental involvement*. This book provides a way for you to help your child get off to a much better start in basic arithmetic. Too many children are left standing at the starting gate, without any notion about which direction to take. This book will help you give your child that direction and smooth the way for an easier time with higher math in high school and college.

Math Foundations for Your First- and Second-Grader is based on a composite of state mathematics curricula. The curricula I followed most closely were those of Indiana, New York, North Carolina, Pennsylvania, and Virginia. Those of California, Connecticut, Florida, Michigan, New Mexico, and Texas were also useful.

It would be nearly impossible for any series of math texts, let alone a single volume, to cover every topic that is taught in every classroom across the nation. So what I've concentrated on are certain core, "must-know" topics. I have identified some two dozen of these core topics that your child must know by the end of the second grade. When your child has learned all of them, he or she will be fully prepared to do more advanced mathematics.

How to Use This Book

This book is divided into two parts. First-grade math is covered in the first half of the book, and second-grade in the second half. The material for each grade is broken into chapters, each covering a basic concept such as counting or simple addition. Each chapter is then broken down into learning modules that I call minilessons. This helps break the material into manageable portions. At the end of each grade there is a final exam. This is not meant to put pressure on your child but to help you identify any trouble spots that may be lingering and to determine whether your child is ready to move on to the math in the next grade. If you are not sure that your child is ready to take the exam, spend more time reviewing and doing practice problems. Be careful to stress that mistakes only mean that you need to spend more time practicing, not that the child has "failed."

Since young children have short attention spans, I suggest you begin by going through the first few minilessons with your child in short spurts. Try to make the sessions fun and pressure-free. Think of games such as awarding points for each correct answer—see how long it takes to get to, say, 50 points. This will encourage your child to continue on and to see the sessions as a fun time for the two of you to spend together rather than as a hated chore.

You may want to try working out each problem yourself rather than just read the solution provided in the book. This may help you better explain to your child how to solve this type of problem.

If you set aside 20 or 30 minutes an evening, four or five evenings a week, you and your child should be able to complete this book in four or five months. Your child has other homework to do as well as a whole life beyond school, so two or three hours a week is plenty of time to spend on math. If it works best for you and your child to set aside a short time to go over one minilesson every weeknight, do that. If you find it works better to wait until the weekend and have one or two longer sessions, that's fine, too. There is no one right way to use this book—except that you should use it consistently to get the most out of it.

At the beginning, your child's reading skills will probably be limited, so you will have to read every word aloud and demonstrate each problem slowly and patiently. As your child becomes able to work more independently, you can either continue to read together or start to allow your child to work alone as you monitor his or her progress. Again, do whatever you find works best for you and your child.

You can probably plan on each minilesson taking 20 to 30 minutes to complete. If the child gets restless, set the book aside and switch to some other activity. Then, some time later, try to get in another 10 or 15 minutes working out more problems. The important part is that the child continues to progress and that you stay patient, emphasizing the thrill of learning. If your child has trouble and you need to repeat a minilesson, try doing this over a number of days and not all at one sitting. There's no need to rush things. Pushing your child too hard will only make you both frustrated and may lead your child to hate math. Remember that no one gets everything right the first time; the trick is to get it right the last time.

You will notice that nearly every page has problems for your child to solve. This is to encourage active learning rather than passive reading. Lead your child through the problems, but be sure that the child is participating and actually understanding the solutions. That way nothing will slip by, with you assuming the child understands. Active learning is harder work but much more effective.

It is important to do the minilessons in the order in which they appear in the book. This is because each new concept builds on the one before, stacking up like a set of building blocks. If the building blocks are not solid, the structure will not be steady. So if your child seems to be struggling, keep on with the concept that is causing the trouble rather than skip it. Try to think of new ways to explain the concept, and keep giving your child more sets of problems to solve. Do not continue on to a new concept until you and your child feel confident that the skill is mastered. Repetition may seem boring, but it really helps to sharpen a child's math skills. I have framed this book around many repetitive drills so that you can be sure your child has the fundamentals down. This can mean working out hundreds of problems.

Again, if your child can't get a concept and starts to act bored, simply stop and return to the math later on. Don't be tempted to skip ahead, because your child needs to build math skills gradually.

As you go on in the book, you'll see that I have included Extra Help boxes that provide review sessions of some of the harder concepts. If your child continues to have trouble, use these boxes for further help. If your child is not having trouble, he or she can skip the box and not be held back.

You'll also notice that I have used many of the dreaded "word problems." If your child gets used to seeing and learning how to solve word problems early on, the later word problems that require more sophisticated thinking will not be so intimidating. Also, word problems help the child see how to use math in real life rather than just blindly applying a formula to a problem. These word problems will help your child begin to use reasoning faculties and instill confidence in his or her problem-solving abilities. So don't skip over these—they are very important.

In times past, books usually referred to all people in the masculine unless obviously referring to females. Since over half the world's population is female, and you are just as likely to be helping a daughter as a son, I will randomly alternate between using *he* and *she* throughout the book. In fact, while math skills are important for both boys and girls, our society tends to discourage girls from excelling in math and science, so you should be extra careful to encourage your daughters to work hard and know that they can be every bit as good as the boys in math.

There is one strict rule that your child should follow: no calculators. I have seen many children become so dependent on these in the early grades that they never learn to *understand* math. Especially in the early grades, understanding the concept is much more important than getting the right answer.

Now you're ready to start. Before you know it, your child will have completed the first two years of math, and I hope you will have had some fun together in the process.

PART I
First-Grade Math

Introduction to First-Grade Math

Chances are, when you went to school, you learned the "old math," as opposed to today's "new math." What's the difference between the old and the new? Don't worry, the answers to the problems haven't changed, but more of an effort is made to have children understand basic concepts rather than just solve problems mechanically.

In the first grade, you'll come across only a few examples of the new math. These will come near the end of the year's work, when your child will learn how to put numbers into groups of 10s and 1s, and when fractions are introduced. Fractions are taught in the first grade? That's right! The new math attempts to introduce more advanced concepts in the early grades so they will be familiar when they are taught in more detail in the later grades. Although this has been somewhat controversial, children are expected to learn something about fractions, a bit of geometry, and a few other concepts in the first two grades.

Will you need to go out and buy any teaching materials? The only things you need are a package of index cards, a deck of playing cards, some coins, paper, and pencils. You might also want to use buttons, blocks, or even dry beans or pasta pieces if seeing and touching these objects helps your child grasp the concepts of the numbers he or she is working with. Let's get started.

Chapter 1

Counting

Counting is the most fundamental mathematical skill. The more advanced skills—arithmetic, algebra, geometry, trigonometry, and higher mathematics—are based on counting. So before we progress with adding and subtracting, it's important to make sure that your child knows how to count. Minilessons 1 through 4 will go over the basics of counting.

MINILESSON 1

Counting to 20

Most children know how to count past 10 by the time they're three. And they just love to show off all their knowledge. First they learn the numbers, without understanding how they're used. Then they point to things and count them. At first they'll make quite a few mistakes, but by the time they're four or five, they usually can count to about 20 and can count objects with reasonable accuracy.

Counting is very basic to mathematics. Before your child enters the first grade, he should definitely be able to count to at least 20 and to count objects with complete accuracy. So what can you do to reinforce your child's ability to count?

When you're out shopping, ask your child: How many people are in line at each checkout counter in the store? At home, how many cans of soup are on the shelf? How many plates are on the dinner table?

Another way of reinforcing your child's knowledge of counting is to encourage abstract counting. That's counting people or things when they're not right there in front of you. How many cousins do you have? How many people live in your house? In the house next door? How many dolls do you have? How many video-tapes?

Point to the balloons in each of the following panels and ask your child, "How many balloons?"

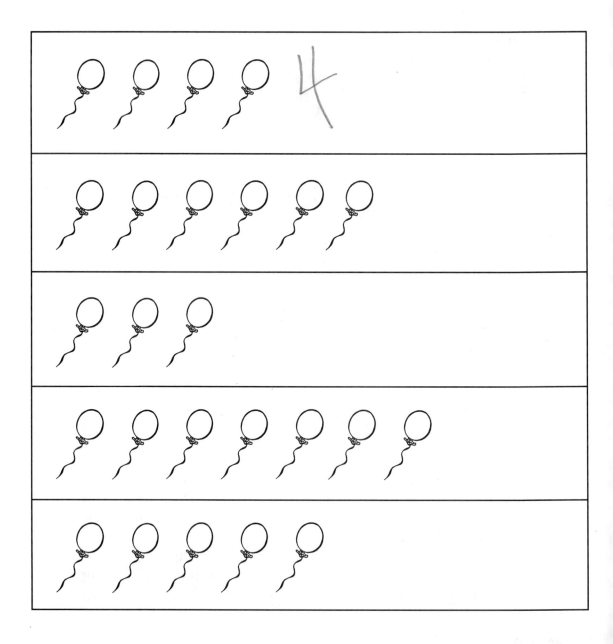

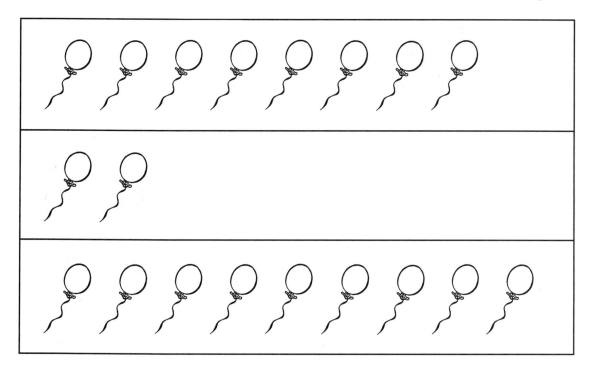

Once your child has gotten these right, it's time to go on to the next minilesson, where you can expand what your child knows about counting.

MINILESSON 2

Counting over 20

How high can your child count? To 20? To 30? Maybe, on a good day, all the way up to 40?

A child entering the first grade should definitely be able to count to 20, but it certainly would not hurt to be able to count higher. Ask your child to count as high as she can. Let's say that your child counts up to 20. "All right," you say, "what comes next?" If she doesn't know, tell her. Then ask her to count from 1 all the way up to 21. If she can't guess what comes next, ask her what comes after 1. And then, what she thinks comes after 21. If things go smoothly, take her all the way up to 29. If they don't, then just let it go and try another day. The lessons should bring you closer to your child rather than frustrate her.

It's very important to pick up where you left off within a day or so. Ask your child to count as high as she can. She'll probably stop where she did earlier, at 20. That doesn't mean that she's completely forgotten 21, 22, and so on, but she either doesn't remember that she actually knows these numbers or doesn't want to make a mistake. After all, she is very confident that she can count to 20, so why take any chances by going beyond the familiar?

Obviously, then, you want to make 21 through 29 very familiar to her. So you ask her to guess what comes after 20. And then after 21. It might help to arrange a line of small objects—coins are my favorite—and have her count these. Point out to her that once you get past 20, it's as though you've gone back to 1 again. If you can count 1, 2, 3, 4, then why not count 21, 22, 23, 24?

Most three-year-olds can manage counting to 10, but they tend to get a little mixed up going much higher. With frequent repetition, they can usually reach 20 without difficulty. Twenty seems to be a plateau where children can get stuck for a while. But once they get past 20, they'll quickly get to 30, 40, 50, and beyond. So if your four- or five-year-old does get stuck at 20, it's important for you and your child not to lose patience. It may take quite a few tries, but then, all of a sudden, your child will break through the barrier.

MINILESSON 3

Recognizing and Reading Numbers up to 40

So far, your child has been counting in his head. Now he's ready to count on paper.

Write the numbers 1 to 40 on a piece of paper. Point to a number and ask, "How much is this?" As long as he keeps getting these numbers right, keep going from number to number. Make a note of any numbers that he gets wrong.

Next, write the numbers 1 to 40, but mix up the sequence. For example, 38, 7, 29, 4, 16... Then ask your child to read each number. See if he can get them all right. He may not be able to on the first try. So keep a record of each number he got wrong.

You'll need to go over each of these numbers with him. If he did get a few wrong, repeat this minilesson the next day and, if necessary, the day after that as well. Remember that most basic math is learned by repetition.

Once you are satisfied that your child has learned to recognize written numbers, it will be time to move on to writing numbers in Minilesson 4.

MINILESSON 4

Writing Numbers over 40

Once your child can count orally and recognize numbers, this knowledge can be further reinforced by having her write the numbers she knows.

Get a piece of paper and a pencil and ask your child to write all the numbers from 1 to 20. Don't worry if a few of the numbers are reversed; for example, if the 6 is written backward. Just remind her how a 6 should look. If she really gets stuck, write the numbers and ask her to copy them until she can write them on her own.

By the time your child enters first grade, she should be able to write the numbers 1 through 20, but it would be better if she could write all the numbers up to 50 or higher. As in Minilesson 2, you might need to point out that once you get above 20, it's just like counting 1, 2, 3, 4 all over again. Another thing you might point out is how we go from 10 to 20 to 30 to 40, which is also like counting from 1 to 2 to 3 to 4, but with 0s on the end.

Once your child can write numbers, she is definitely ready for more advanced work. But you can help reinforce the number-writing skill by having her write out all the numbers up to 50 once every week or two.

Counting puts a child at ease with numbers. Instead of intimidating mathematical symbols, they become familiar objects, often associated with very pleasant memories. Try counting at least a few times a week with your child. Throw a pile of buttons on the table and tell your child to count them, or ask her to count her stuffed animals or books. Count different objects to keep the child from getting bored. Once counting to 50 is mastered, your child will be ready for addition and then subtraction.

Chapter 2

Adding Single-Digit Numbers

The numbers 1, 2, 3, 4, 5, 6, 7, 8, and 9 are single-digit numbers. Single-digit numbers have just one number, while double-digit numbers have two numbers, like 35 and 21. In Minilessons 5 through 7, we'll be adding single-digit numbers. As we work our way through the book, we'll be adding double-digit numbers.

MINILESSON 5

From Counting to Adding

Learning to count leads to learning to add. There are two easy ways to teach addition. The first is to add two groups of objects, and the second is to count measured distances along a number line.

Adding Two Groups of Objects

Look at the circles below. Ask your child, "If we add these three circles to these two circles, how many circles do we get?"

If your child tells you the answer is 5, go on to the next problem. If your child needs help, count the circles with her:

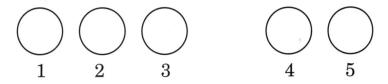

1   2   3   4   5

15

Here's another problem: How much are four boxes plus three boxes?

Again, just count the boxes:

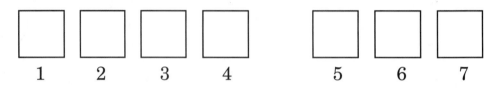

Do this problem with circles: 3 + 3 = _____.

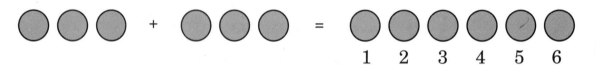

Now try one without the circles: 4 + 1 = _____. Show your child that 4 + 1 is the same thing as adding four circles and one circle, and then counting up the circles:

Next, ask your child to find the answer to this problem by drawing circles below: 1 + 3 = _____.

Did your child draw four circles and get the answer 4? Good.
Here's one more: 2 + 2 = _____.

Did we get 4? Good. So keep reminding your child whenever she
gets stuck adding single-digit numbers that she just needs to
draw some circles, put them together, and count them up, and
she'll always get the right answer.

Adding on a Number Line

Ask your child, "How much is 5 plus 2?" If she answers, "7," go
on to the next problem. But if your child needs some help, then
use the number line below.

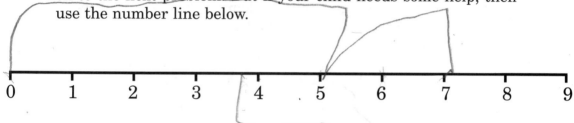

Have your child start at 0 and move five spaces to 5. Then count
up two more spaces. Where did she land?

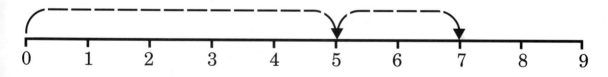

Here's one more: Ask, "How much is 4 plus 5?" If your child
says, "9," go on to the next minilesson. If she is unsure, use the
number line below.

Tell her to start at 0 and count to 4. Then continue counting for another five spaces. Where did she land?

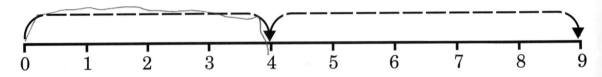

MINILESSON 6

Addition Tables: Part 1

By now your child has added circles and squares and counted spaces along a line. What about rote learning? What about memorizing an entire addition table, like the one below?

TABLE 1

Addition of 1 + 1 to 5 + 5

+	1	2	3	4	5
1	2	3	4	5	6
2	3	4	5	6	7
3	4	5	6	7	8
4	5	6	7	8	9
5	6	7	8	9	10

Your child may not see addition tables in school because memorization has been de-emphasized. But I believe that memorization does have its benefits if it is used wisely.

Table 1 shows all the sums from 1 + 1 up to 5 + 5. Go over the table with your child. Start at the plus sign (+) in the upper left-hand corner of the table. Just below the plus sign is 1. You'll also find a 1 to the right of the plus sign. Adding the 1 below the plus sign and the 1 to the right of the plus sign, we get 2. What we really did was a box step: We went from the 1 below the plus sign up to the plus sign, then to the 1 to the right of the plus sign, then down to the number to the right of the starting number. So, 1 + 1 = 2.

Now show your child 4 + 3. Start with the 4 that is directly below the plus sign. Again, do the box step: Go from the 4 up to the plus sign, then to the 3 to the right of the plus sign, and then down to the number to the right of the starting number. So 4 + 3 = 7. You'll notice that the 7 is on the same row as the 4 and in the same column as the 3.

One more box step: What is 5 + 5? Start with the 5 in the lower left-hand corner of the table, go up to the plus sign, then to the 5 in the upper right-hand corner, and finally, go down to the number to the right of the starting number: 5 + 5 = 10.

In order to add correctly, your child has to learn all the combinations of numbers in Table 1. Chances are, he knows most or all of them already. How do you find out for sure? Have your child try these problems.

Problem Set A

1. 1 + 2 = 3
2. 2 + 4 = 6
3. 5 + 2 = 7
4. 3 + 2 = 5
5. 4 + 4 = 8
6. 1 + 5 = 6
7. 3 + 3 = 6
8. 2 + 5 = 7
9. 4 + 1 = 5
10. 5 + 4 = 9
11. 4 + 3 = 7
12. 5 + 5 = 10
13. 1 + 3 = 4
14. 2 + 3 = 5
15. 5 + 3 = 8

Answers on page 23.

Don't worry if your child relies on counting on his fingers to answer these. As long as he gets the right answer, it's okay at this point if he takes off his shoes and socks and counts on his toes as well.

Remember that addition is an extension of counting. Once your child has mastered the addition tables, he won't need to count on his fingers—or his toes.

If your child got each problem right, then go on to Minilesson 7. If not, then there's still work to be done right here. But wait an hour or even a day if your child is getting frustrated.

Write down each problem that your child got wrong. If he missed only one, then it shouldn't take long for him to learn it. But if he got three or four wrong, go back to the beginning of Minilesson 5, and then return to this one. Keep using the addition table. Sometimes it takes a while to learn all of it, but it's time well spent. Before going on to Minilesson 7, make sure your child can get every one of the problems in Minilesson 6 right.

If your child continues to struggle with the addition table, try another tack. Drop everything for a while. Later or the next day start with a list of every problem that's giving your child trouble and have him draw objects so that he can *see* the addition. Or work with concrete objects such as dry pasta pieces or peanuts, since many young children need to touch and feel what they count.

Let's say that your child is having trouble with 6 + 4 and 7 + 3. To do the first problem, have your child draw six triangles, a plus sign, and then four more triangles:

Now ask him to add the triangles. If he got it right, then go on to the next problem. If not, tell him to count the triangles:

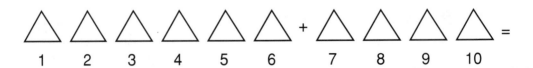

Remind him that addition is really just counting. So adding these triangles is as easy as counting from 1 to 10.

Next problem: Have your child draw seven triangles, a plus sign, and then three more triangles, like this:

△ △ △ △ △ △ △ + △ △ △ =

Now ask him to count or add the triangles.

△ △ △ △ △ △ △ + △ △ △ =
1 2 3 4 5 6 7   8 9 10

MINILESSON 7

Addition Tables: Part 2

So far we've added as high as 5 + 5. Table 2 takes us up to 9 + 5. Go over this table with your child for a few minutes. Start with 6 + 1, and then 6 + 2, 6 + 3, 6 + 4, and 6 + 5. Then do the 7s, the 8s, and the 9s rows.

TABLE 2
Addition of 6 + 1 to 9 + 5

+	1	2	3	4	5
6	7	8	9	10	11
7	8	9	10	11	12
8	9	10	11	12	13
9	10	11	12	13	14

It's important that your child memorize this table. Keep going over it until he's comfortable with it. If necessary, use the drawing trick described in Minilesson 6 for any he can't remember. Once he seems to know the table fairly well, use flash cards to practice with him.

To make the flash cards, you'll need a package of ruled index cards or just cut-up pieces of thick paper. Let your child help you. This can be a fun activity as well as more practice with numbers.

Copy Problem Set B on the ruled side of the index cards. As you do each card, write the answer on the back. Show cards one by one to your child and ask him to tell you the answers. If he gets any wrong, help him figure out the answers by drawing circles or using his fingers. Put aside the cards he gets wrong.

After you've gone through the whole stack, take the cards he got wrong and ask him to try them again. If he keeps getting certain problems wrong, go back to the table. But remember to keep the tone light. Treat this as a game in which it's much better to try than not to try, even if this means making mistakes.

You may be asking yourself, is all this memorization really necessary? I'll tell you why it is. Mathematical reasoning is impossible without having a good feel for numbers. Unless a child learns addition and subtraction in the first grade, it becomes very hard to progress any further. The children who get turned off by math are not those who had to memorize addition tables, but those who didn't.

Numbers can be very intimidating to older children, but they won't be to those who get comfortable with them in the first grade. Familiarity is said to breed contempt, but in mathematics it breeds competence.

Problem Set B

1. $7 + 2 =$ _____
2. $9 + 4 =$ _____
3. $6 + 1 =$ _____
4. $3 + 6 =$ _____
5. $5 + 9 =$ _____
6. $7 + 4 =$ _____

7. $6 + 5 =$ _____
8. $5 + 8 =$ _____
9. $7 + 3 =$ _____
10. $1 + 7 =$ _____
11. $9 + 3 =$ _____
12. $1 + 8 =$ _____

13. $8 + 3 =$ _____
14. $9 + 5 =$ _____
15. $4 + 6 =$ _____
16. $4 + 8 =$ _____
17. $3 + 7 =$ _____
18. $4 + 7 =$ _____

Answers below.

If your child gets all of them correct, he's ready for subtraction. If not, keep using the flash cards and Table 2 until he has it down pat.

Answers to Chapter 2 Problem Sets

Problem Set A

1. 3	5. 8	9. 5	13. 4
2. 6	6. 6	10. 9	14. 5
3. 7	7. 6	11. 7	15. 8
4. 5	8. 7	12. 10	

Problem Set B

1. 9	6. 11	11. 12	16. 12
2. 13	7. 11	12. 9	17. 10
3. 7	8. 13	13. 11	18. 11
4. 9	9. 10	14. 14	
5. 14	10. 8	15. 10	

Chapter 3

Subtracting Single-Digit Numbers

You can start out by explaining to your child that subtraction is the mathematical opposite of addition. When you add two numbers, you end up with a number that is larger than either of the two numbers you started with. When you start with one number and subtract another number, you end up with a smaller number than the one you started with.

For example, ask your child, "How much is 2 plus 2?" By now, she should be able to tell you it's 4. Point out that 4 is more than 2. Now ask, "How much is 4 take away 2?" She may not know, so tell her the answer is 2, and point out that 2 is less than 4. In Minilessons 8 through 10, your child will get plenty of practice doing subtraction problems.

MINILESSON 8

Simple Subtraction: Part 1

Ask your child to line up five ordinary playing cards, facedown. Or use any other objects that are handy. Now ask, "How much is 5 take away 3?" If your child is stuck, have her count the five cards. Then take three cards away and ask, "How many cards are left?"

Now have your child line up four cards. Ask her, "How much is 4 take away 1?" Again, if she gets stuck, take away one card and ask her how many cards are left.

Try the same strategy with 5 take away 2.

Now you're both on a roll. So keep asking questions:

How much is 4 take away 3?
How much is 5 take away 1?
How much is 3 take away 2?
How much is 4 take away 2?

Once your child is confident with this, vary it a bit by asking, "How much is 3 minus 1?" Explain that minus is another way of saying "take away." Ask her these questions:

How much is 2 minus 1?
How much is 5 minus 4?
How much is 5 minus 3?

If your child is getting everything right, ask her to try the problem set below. If not, then use the Extra Help box.

Problem Set A

1. $3 - 1 = $ _____   **4.** $5 - 4 = $ _____   **7.** $5 - 3 = $ _____

2. $5 - 1 = $ _____   **5.** $4 - 1 = $ _____   **8.** $3 - 2 = $ _____

3. $4 - 2 = $ _____   **6.** $2 - 1 = $ _____   **9.** $4 - 3 = $ _____

Answers on page 31.

If your child got each of these right, then go directly to Minilesson 9. If not, then go over the Extra Help box with your child.

Subtraction

Subtracting one set of objects from another

Ask your child, "How much is 8 minus 3?" Even if your child gives you the correct answer of 5, ask him to draw eight houses like those below.

Then have him cross out three of the houses:

Ask him how many houses are left.

Subtracting distances

Now ask, "How much is 7 minus 4?" Whether or not you get 3 for an answer, show him this line:

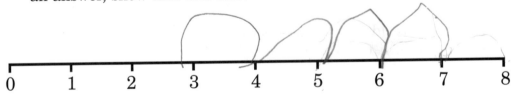

Ask your child to start at 7 and move his finger four spaces to the left. Where did he land? Show him the line below.

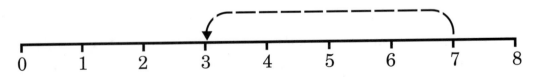

This time we'll use boxes. To find out how much 5 – 2 is, draw five boxes:

Then subtract, or take away, two:

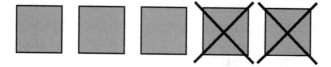

That leaves us with three boxes:

Ask your child to use boxes to find out what 4 – 1 is.

Did your child draw four boxes and take away one of them, like this?

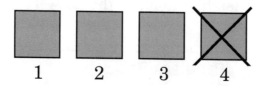

1   2   3   4

If so, he probably got the answer 3.
   Let's try one more, using boxes. What is 5 – 3?

Did your child get 2? I hope so. If you start with five boxes and take away three, then you're left with two boxes.

Simple Subtraction: Part 2

This minilesson is a continuation of the last one, but now we'll use bigger numbers. Have your child line up seven playing cards, seven pennies, or seven other objects that you can put your hands on. Ask, "How much is 7 take away 2?" If he gets stuck, take away two cards and ask, "Now, how much is 7 take away 2?"

Have your child line up the seven cards again. How much is 7 take away 4? If necessary, take away the four cards and let him count how many are left.

Now have your child line up eight cards. How much is 8 take away 6?

Now line up six cards. How much is 6 minus 3?

Line up nine cards. How much is 9 minus 4?

Once your child can answer these questions correctly, start asking questions without telling him to line up the cards:

How much is 8 take away 5?
How much is 7 take away 3?
How much is 9 minus 2?
How much is 6 minus 4?
How much is 8 take away 2?

If your child could handle those, it's time for him to do a little work independently. Ask him to fill in the answers to the equations below.

Problem Set B		
1. $6 - 1 = \underline{5}$	**5.** $6 - 5 = \underline{1}$	**9.** $6 - 3 = \underline{3}$
2. $8 - 3 = \underline{}$	**6.** $8 - 1 = \underline{7}$	**10.** $7 - 5 = \underline{2}$
3. $9 - 4 = \underline{}$	**7.** $9 - 6 = \underline{3}$	**11.** $7 - 1 = \underline{6}$
4. $7 - 4 = \underline{}$	**8.** $9 - 8 = \underline{1}$	**12.** $8 - 2 = \underline{6}$

Answers on page 31.

If your child got everything right, then he's ready for Minilesson 10. If not, review the problems he got wrong. Let's say he missed 9 – 4 and 8 – 2.

To figure out 9 – 4, have your child draw nine triangles like this:

Ask him to make sure there are nine. What he'll do, of course, is count them. Now ask him to take away four by crossing out four triangles, like this:

Now ask him, "How many triangles are left?" He can count to find out that there are five.

Next problem: How much is 8 – 2? Ask your child to draw eight triangles (or circles or squares), like this:

Now take away two:

How many are left? Clearly, six are left.

MINILESSON 10

Simple Subtraction: Part 3

Here's a card game you can use to teach subtraction. This game is closely related to the card game called War. In War you use the face cards and the ace is the highest card on the table. In the game I'm about to describe, we'll have the ace count as one, and we'll remove the face cards and 10s, so we'll be using cards from 1 to 9. Whoever has the higher card takes the other player's card. If there's a tie, you can break it the way you do in War—each player places four cards facedown and turns a fifth card faceup. The winner takes all the cards that are down.

Now let's play cards. Remove the joker, face cards (kings, queens, and jacks), and 10s from a deck of playing cards. Deal out all the cards facedown into two piles, one for you and one for your child. Then you each turn over your top card. Let's say that yours is a 9 and your child's is a 6. "Whose card is higher?" you ask. If he gets that right, ask, "How much higher is my card?" If your child gets stuck, you can ask, "How much is mine?... And how much is yours?" And then, "How much is 9 take away 6?"

If your child still isn't sure, use the 9 card to show how 9 take away 6 is 3. If it's a 9 of Diamonds, cover six of the diamonds and ask how many are left.

Work your way through the rest of the deck like this. Remember, it's a game, but no one's keeping score.

When you've finished the deck, ask your child to work out these problems. Be sure to check the answers.

Problem Set C

1. $8 - 4 =$ ____
2. $6 - 1 =$ ____
3. $4 - 3 =$ ____
4. $7 - 2 =$ ____
5. $5 - 1 =$ ____

6. $8 - 2 =$ ____
7. $9 - 4 =$ ____
8. $7 - 5 =$ ____
9. $9 - 2 =$ ____
10. $6 - 3 =$ ____

11. $8 - 3 =$ ____
12. $9 - 7 =$ ____
13. $7 - 1 =$ ____
14. $5 - 3 =$ ____
15. $8 - 6 =$ ____

Answers on page 31.

If he gets them all right, proceed to Minilesson 11. Otherwise, help your child figure out the correct answers. Begin with the problems that he got wrong. Suppose one was 8 – 4. Ask him to draw eight circles like this:

Ask your child, "How much is 8 take away 4?" Have the child cover or cross out four of the circles and count those that remain to get the right answer. Use this method on any of the other problems that he missed.

Now copy all the problems over and have your child do them again. If two or more are wrong, then have him do each of those problems by drawing circles.

You may be thinking, Shouldn't the child be able to do these problems in his head, without drawing circles? That would be ideal, but many children need to see things literally before they can think about them abstractly. Think of the circles as training wheels on a bicycle that are eventually discarded.

Answers to Chapter 3 Problem Sets

Problem Set A

1. 2	**4.** 1	**7.** 2
2. 4	**5.** 3	**8.** 1
3. 2	**6.** 1	**9.** 1

Problem Set B

1. 5	**4.** 3	**7.** 3	**10.** 2
2. 5	**5.** 1	**8.** 1	**11.** 6
3. 5	**6.** 7	**9.** 3	**12.** 6

Problem Set C

1. 4	**5.** 4	**9.** 7	**13.** 6
2. 5	**6.** 6	**10.** 3	**14.** 2
3. 1	**7.** 5	**11.** 5	**15.** 2
4. 5	**8.** 2	**12.** 2	

Chapter 4

Building Math Skills

So far we've worked on three very fundamental mathematical tools: counting, adding, and subtracting. Now we'll work on three skills that will help your child to use those tools. First we'll look at the relationship between words and numbers in Minilesson 11, then at the concept of 0 (zero) in Minilesson 12, and finally, at filling in the missing number in Minilesson 13.

MINILESSON 11

Translating Words into Numbers

Reading and arithmetic skills are very closely related. Children with reading problems usually have trouble with math, especially when they need to follow written instructions. While all we can do here is help you teach your child math, it is extremely important for you to monitor your child's progress in learning to read.

Perhaps the best way of doing this is to have your child read to you, while you help her pronounce difficult words and correct her mistakes. In this minilesson we'll begin connecting words with numbers. By now your child should be able to write the words that go with each number up to 10. Can your child do this? Let's find out. Ask her to write the words for each of the numbers listed below.

1 _____   6 _____

2 _____   7 _____

3 _____   8 _____

4 _____   9 _____

5 _____   10 _____

Did your child get all these right? If she did, you can go on to Minilesson 12. If she didn't, then try this exercise.

Write the number that goes with each of these words:

one	_____	six	_____
two	_____	seven	_____
three	_____	eight	_____
four	_____	nine	_____
five	_____	ten	_____

If she's still having trouble matching words with numbers, ask her to write the words for the numbers 1 to 10. Then ask her to read each number.

Once she's done this, have her take another shot at the previous exercise, writing the numbers next to each of the words from one to ten. If she still can't do this, she may have trouble reading rather than trouble with math. Many students who do poorly in math have reading problems, which makes it hard for them to understand what they're being asked to do. Although this goes well beyond the scope of this book, I suggest that if you think your child is having any difficulty reading, you take about 15 minutes every night and have your child read to you, so you can correct any mistakes.

MINILESSON 12

Introducing the Concept of 0 (Zero)

Some children initially have a problem with the number 0. How much is it? One less than 1? Nothing?

The real problem with 0 is that it's an abstract term. You can't see it. You can't touch it. You can't represent it with a penny, a button, or a slice of pie. It's just lying out there somewhere, and a lot of children aren't sure just what to make of it.

I find that the best way to demystify most mathematical concepts is to use them in problems. Start out by putting three pennies on your outstretched palm. Ask the child how many pennies you have in your hand. Then put two pennies in your hand and ask him how many pennies are in your hand. Then do it with one penny. And then do it with *no* pennies.

After your child answers, "No pennies," go back to the three pennies. On a piece of paper, ask him to write the number 3. Next, ask him to write the numbers 2 and 1. And then ask, "If we have no pennies, how do we write a number for that?" He probably won't know, so show him by writing the number 0. Explain that 0 represents zero pennies, or no pennies. If we have three bottles, we write 3, but if we have zero bottles, or no bottles, we write 0.

Now we're ready to do a little addition. Ask your child, how much is one penny plus one penny? And then, how much is one penny plus zero pennies?

The number 0 is very important in mathematics. In the first grade, however, your child needs to know just three things about 0. The first is that when 0 is added to another number, nothing changes. For example, $4 + 0 = 4$. The second is that when 0 is subtracted from a number, nothing changes: $9 - 0 = 9$. The third "zero fact" your child should know is that 0 is the answer to the general question, How much is a number minus that same number? For example, how much is $5 - 5$? How much is $7 - 7$? And how much is $3 - 3$?

Some children grasp adding with 0s almost instinctively, but others need concrete illustrations. So try asking your child, "How much is one penny plus zero pennies?"

Then ask, "How much is 3 plus 0?" Again, if your child isn't sure, use the pennies to provide a concrete example.

Now have your child complete these problems:

Problem Set A

1. $2 + 0 =$ ___2___ **4.** $0 + 3 =$ ___3___ **7.** $8 + 0 =$ ___8___

2. $4 + 0 =$ ___4___ **5.** $6 + 0 =$ ___6___ **8.** $0 + 5 =$ ___5___

3. $0 + 1 =$ _____ **6.** $0 + 4 =$ ___4___ **9.** $0 + 0 =$ _____

Answers on page 37.

Did he get everything right? If not, go over with him each problem that he got wrong. And then have him try the whole set over again. Once you're sure he can add with 0s, see how he can handle subtraction. Have him do this set of problems.

Problem Set B

1. $3 - 0 =$ ___ 3

2. $1 - 1 =$ ___ 0

3. $4 - 0 =$ ___ 4

4. $3 - 3 =$ ___ 0

5. $5 - 0 =$ ___

6. $0 - 0 =$ ___

7. $2 - 2 =$ ___

8. $6 - 0 =$ ___ 6

9. $5 - 5 =$ ___ 0

Answers on page 37.

If he got any wrong, try the penny exercise to illustrate the point. Then go over each one he missed. Once he gets them all right, go onward to missing numbers in Minilesson 13.

MINILESSON 13

Filling in the Missing Number

Ask your child to fill in the blank:

$$2 + \underline{}_{2} = 4$$

The missing number is 2.

And now ask your child to fill in the missing number in this problem:

$$1 + \underline{}_{3} = 4$$

The missing number is 3.

Here's one more:

$$3 + \underline{}_{2} = 5$$

The missing number is 2.

Filling in the missing number is one of those exercises that stretch your child's mathematical imagination. Have your child fill in the blanks in the first set of problems below. If she gets no more than one or two wrong, then move along to Minilesson 14. But if she gets more than two problems wrong, just wait till tomorrow, and then try this minilesson over again, this time doing both problem sets.

Problem Set C

1. $3 + \underline{3} = 6$
2. $2 + \underline{2} = 4$
3. $8 + \underline{1} = 9$
4. $4 + \underline{0} = 4$
5. $7 + \underline{2} = 9$
6. $5 + \underline{2} = 7$

7. $2 + \underline{5} = 7$
8. $6 + \underline{3} = 9$
9. $4 + \underline{4} = 8$
10. $1 + \underline{6} = 7$
11. $3 + \underline{2} = 5$
12. $0 + \underline{6} = 6$

13. $2 + \underline{7} = 9$
14. $5 + \underline{1} = 6$
15. $1 + \underline{7} = 8$
16. $3 + \underline{5} = 8$
17. $8 + \underline{0} = 8$
18. $0 + \underline{9} = 9$

Answers on page 37.

Problem Set D

1. $4 - \underline{1} = 3$
2. $8 - 1 = \underline{7}$
3. $6 - \underline{4} = 2$
4. $9 - \underline{5} = 4$
5. $3 - \underline{1} = 2$
6. $1 - \underline{0} = 1$

7. $8 - \underline{2} = 6$
8. $5 - \underline{1} = 4$
9. $0 - \underline{0} = 0$
10. $6 - \underline{3} = 3$
11. $5 - \underline{4} = 1$
12. $8 - \underline{6} = 2$

13. $9 - \underline{9} = 0$
14. $7 - \underline{4} = 3$
15. $4 - \underline{1} = 3$
16. $2 - \underline{1} = 1$
17. $3 - \underline{2} = 1$
18. $1 - \underline{1} = 0$

Answers on page 37.

If your child got more than two wrong in either problem set, it may be a signal that her addition and subtraction skills are not yet well enough developed to go any further right now. The best thing to do is to repeat Minilessons 6 through 10 for a few weeks, and then take another look at this minilesson.

Answers to Chapter 4 Problem Sets

Problem Set A

1. 2	4. 3	7. 8
2. 4	5. 6	8. 5
3. 1	6. 4	9. 0

Problem Set B

1. 3	4. 0	7. 0
2. 0	5. 5	8. 6
3. 4	6. 0	9. 0

Problem Set C

1. 3	6. 2	11. 2	16. 5
2. 2	7. 5	12. 6	17. 0
3. 1	8. 3	13. 7	18. 9
4. 0	9. 4	14. 1	
5. 2	10. 6	15. 7	

Problem Set D

1. 1	6. 0	11. 4	16. 1
2. 7	7. 2	12. 6	17. 2
3. 4	8. 1	13. 9	18. 1
4. 5	9. 0	14. 4	
5. 1	10. 3	15. 1	

Chapter 5

Addition and Subtraction Drills

This chapter has two purposes. The first is to test your child's knowledge of addition and subtraction before we go on to the more advanced work in adding and subtracting. The second is to provide a review of much of what we have covered over the last nine minilessons.

MINILESSON 14

Addition Drills

As I never get tired of repeating, a lot of math is learned by repetition. So here's a chance to take a break and let your child do some work on her own.

Here are three addition drills. If your child is able to work completely on her own, she can check her own answers. But it would probably be a good idea for you to check her work as well, to make sure she really knows her addition.

If she gets any problems wrong, review them with her. If you find it helps, use pennies or some other objects to help her to literally *see* addition taking place.

Problem Set A

1. $2 + 1 = $ _3_

2. $0 + 2 = $ _2_

3. $3 + 1 = $ _4_

4. $0 + 1 = $ ____

5. $4 + 1 = $ ____

6. $2 + 2 = $ ____

7. $4 + 0 = $ ____

8. $1 + 2 = $ ____

9. $3 + 2 = $ ____

10. $1 + 3 = $ ____

11. $0 + 3 = $ ____

12. $2 + 0 = $ ____

13. $1 + 1 = $ ____

14. $0 + 0 = $ ____

15. $1 + 4 = $ ____

16. $1 + 0 = $ ____

17. $0 + 4 = $ ____

18. $3 + 0 = $ ____

Answers on page 43.

Problem Set B

1. $1 + 6 = $ ____

2. $4 + 3 = $ ____

3. $6 + 0 = $ ____

4. $5 + 3 = $ ____

5. $4 + 2 = $ ____

6. $7 + 1 = $ ____

7. $0 + 6 = $ ____

8. $2 + 5 = $ ____

9. $6 + 1 = $ ____

10. $5 + 1 = $ ____

11. $3 + 3 = $ ____

12. $6 + 2 = $ ____

13. $0 + 7 = $ ____

14. $3 + 5 = $ ____

15. $4 + 1 = $ ____

16. $2 + 6 = $ ____

17. $3 + 4 = $ ____

18. $7 + 0 = $ ____

19. $0 + 8 = $ ____

20. $1 + 5 = $ ____

21. $2 + 4 = $ ____

22. $0 + 5 = $ ____

23. $1 + 7 = $ ____

24. $4 + 4 = $ ____

Answers on page 44.

Problem Set C

1. $0 + 8 =$ _____   8. $2 + 7 =$ _____   15. $1 + 8 =$ _____

2. $7 + 2 =$ _____   9. $7 + 1 =$ _____   16. $2 + 5 =$ _____

3. $1 + 6 =$ _____   10. $8 + 0 =$ _____   17. $1 + 7 =$ _____

4. $6 + 2 =$ _____   11. $4 + 4 =$ _____   18. $0 + 9 =$ _____

5. $9 + 0 =$ _____   12. $1 + 5 =$ _____   19. $8 + 1 =$ _____

6. $5 + 3 =$ _____   13. $6 + 3 =$ _____   20. $5 + 4 =$ _____

7. $4 + 5 =$ _____   14. $2 + 6 =$ _____   21. $3 + 6 =$ _____

Answers on page 44.

If your child got everything right in these problem sets, then skip the rest of this minilesson and go directly to Minilesson 15.

If your child got one or more problems wrong, go over those problems very carefully. Let's say she got 4 + 5 wrong. Put nine pennies on the kitchen table in groups of four and five. Ask your daughter to add the two groups. Then put nine spoons on the table in groups of four and five. It won't take long for her to get the message: 4 + 5 = 9.

Follow exactly the same procedure for any other problems she missed. Once that's done, have her redo the problem sets in Minilesson 7. This time she'll almost definitely get them all right.

If she still gets some wrong, give her some time away from math, then repeat this minilesson. Then go on to Minilesson 15.

MINILESSON 15

Subtraction Drills

This minilesson contains two problem sets. If your child gets more than one wrong in Problem Set D, then you'll need to have him do the work in the Extra Help box before he moves on to Problem Set E.

Problem Set D

1. $7 - 7 =$ _____
2. $8 - 2 =$ _____
3. $6 - 0 =$ _____
4. $9 - 4 =$ _____
5. $6 - 3 =$ _____
6. $7 - 1 =$ _____
7. $8 - 3 =$ _____
8. $9 - 6 =$ _____
9. $7 - 6 =$ _____
10. $6 - 4 =$ _____

11. $7 - 0 =$ _____
12. $6 - 1 =$ _____
13. $8 - 4 =$ _____
14. $9 - 5 =$ _____
15. $7 - 2 =$ _____
16. $8 - 5 =$ _____
17. $7 - 3 =$ _____
18. $9 - 1 =$ _____
19. $8 - 6 =$ _____
20. $9 - 8 =$ _____

21. $6 - 2 =$ _____
22. $7 - 4 =$ _____
23. $9 - 0 =$ _____
24. $8 - 1 =$ _____
25. $6 - 5 =$ _____
26. $8 - 7 =$ _____
27. $9 - 9 =$ _____
28. $7 - 5 =$ _____
29. $6 - 6 =$ _____
30. $9 - 7 =$ _____

Answers on page 44.

EXTRA HELP

Subtraction

If your child is still having trouble subtracting, tell him not to worry if subtraction takes a while. With practice, he'll get it. There are two ways he can get his subtraction down. One way is to draw circles, boxes, or triangles. The other way is to memorize every combination of numbers. If he does enough subtraction (and addition) problems, he will end up memorizing these combinations and getting them right. Have him try again, this time using triangles.

Let's work out this problem using triangles:

$$9 - 3 = \underline{\hspace{1.5cm}}$$

First draw nine triangles:

Then take away three:

How many are left?

Now ask your child to draw triangles to find the answer to this problem:

$$8 - 2 = \underline{\hspace{1.5cm}}$$

Here's how the triangles should have come out:

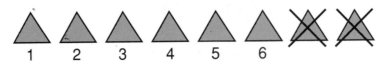

One last problem:

$$7 - 4 = \underline{\hspace{1.5cm}}$$

The answer is 3.

Problem Set E

1. $7 - 6$ = _____
2. $10 - 2$ = _____
3. $9 - 5$ = _____
4. $4 - 1$ = _____
5. $8 - 1$ = _____
6. $10 - 6$ = _____
7. $6 - 2$ = _____
8. $7 - 2$ = _____
9. $10 - 4$ = _____
10. $5 - 2$ = _____
11. $10 - 5$ = _____
12. $9 - 1$ = _____
13. $9 - 3$ = _____
14. $7 - 5$ = _____
15. $2 - 1$ = _____

16. $9 - 4$ = _____
17. $6 - 1$ = _____
18. $7 - 3$ = _____
19. $5 - 4$ = _____
20. $3 - 2$ = _____
21. $9 - 2$ = _____
22. $9 - 6$ = _____
23. $5 - 3$ = _____
24. $10 - 3$ = _____
25. $10 - 1$ = _____
26. $4 - 2$ = _____
27. $8 - 6$ = _____
28. $8 - 5$ = _____
29. $8 - 2$ = _____
30. $8 - 3$ = _____

31. $8 - 4$ = _____
32. $6 - 4$ = _____
33. $7 - 4$ = _____
34. $4 - 3$ = _____
35. $10 - 8$ = _____
36. $8 - 7$ = _____
37. $3 - 1$ = _____
38. $9 - 7$ = _____
39. $6 - 3$ = _____
40. $7 - 1$ = _____
41. $10 - 9$ = _____
42. $6 - 5$ = _____
43. $5 - 1$ = _____
44. $10 - 7$ = _____
45. $9 - 8$ = _____

Answers on page 44.

Answers to Chapter 5 Problem Sets

Problem Set A

1. 3	6. 4	11. 3	16. 1
2. 2	7. 4	12. 2	17. 4
3. 4	8. 3	13. 2	18. 3
4. 1	9. 5	14. 0	
5. 5	10. 4	15. 5	

Problem Set B

1. 7	7. 6	13. 7	19. 8
2. 7	8. 7	14. 8	20. 6
3. 6	9. 7	15. 5	21. 6
4. 8	10. 6	16. 8	22. 5
5. 6	11. 6	17. 7	23. 8
6. 8	12. 8	18. 7	24. 8

Problem Set C

1. 8	7. 9	13. 9	19. 9
2. 9	8. 9	14. 8	20. 9
3. 7	9. 8	15. 9	21. 9
4. 8	10. 8	16. 7	
5. 9	11. 8	17. 8	
6. 8	12. 6	18. 9	

Problem Set D

1. 0	9. 1	17. 4	25. 1
2. 6	10. 2	18. 8	26. 1
3. 6	11. 7	19. 2	27. 0
4. 5	12. 5	20. 1	28. 2
5. 3	13. 4	21. 4	29. 0
6. 6	14. 4	22. 3	30. 2
7. 5	15. 5	23. 9	
8. 3	16. 3	24. 7	

Problem Set E

1. 1	13. 6	25. 9	37. 2
2. 8	14. 2	26. 2	38. 2
3. 4	15. 1	27. 2	39. 3
4. 3	16. 5	28. 3	40. 6
5. 7	17. 5	29. 6	41. 1
6. 4	18. 4	30. 5	42. 1
7. 4	19. 1	31. 4	43. 4
8. 5	20. 1	32. 2	44. 3
9. 6	21. 7	33. 3	45. 1
10. 3	22. 3	34. 1	
11. 5	23. 2	35. 2	
12. 8	24. 7	36. 1	

Chapter 6

Addition into Double Digits

So far your child has been adding just two numbers. This chapter will take her beyond that. In Minilesson 16 we'll progress to adding three numbers. And then, in Minilesson 17, we will be adding numbers whose sum is greater than 9. These numbers, like 12, 15, and 18, are double-digit numbers. By the time you finish the chapter, your child will be quite familiar with double-digit numbers.

MINILESSON 16

Adding Three Numbers

When your child has the addition tables memorized, adding three numbers is just an extension of adding two. For instance, take the problem:

$$4 + 2 + 3 = ?$$

Ask your child, "How much is 4 plus 2?" If she gets that right, ask, "How much is 6 plus 3?" Explain that you add the first two numbers, 4 + 2, and get 6. Then you take that number, 6, and add 3 to it, getting 9.

Make sure your child understands the process; then have your child add these numbers:

$$3 + 2 + 2 = ?$$

If your child gets this right, go on to the next problem. If not, try explaining it this way:

Just add up the boxes:

☐ ☐ ☐ + ☐ ☐ = how many boxes?

There are five. Now add these:

☐ ☐ ☐ ☐ ☐ + ☐ ☐ = how many boxes?

There are seven. The answer to 3 + 2 + 2 is 7.
   Next question:

$$2 + 3 + 3 = ?$$

Again, if your child got the correct answer, 8, go directly to
Problem Set A and have your child work each of these problems.
If your child needs more help, break down 2 + 3 + 3 into two parts
and use boxes. Have your child add these boxes:

☐ ☐ + ☐ ☐ ☐ =

The answer is 5. Then have her add these:

☐ ☐ ☐ ☐ ☐ + ☐ ☐ ☐ =

Did she get 8 this time?
   If your child needs a little more assistance in adding three
numbers, use the Extra Help box. If not, go directly to Problem
Set A and ask her to work on the problems. Be sure to check her
work.

Adding Three Numbers

Help your child work out how to add these three numbers:

$$2 + 2 + 4 = ?$$

First we add 2 + 2 and get 4. Next we add 4 + 4 and get 8.
   Now here's another one to go through with your child:

$$3 + 4 + 2 = ?$$

First we add 3 + 4 and get 7. Next, how much is 7 + 2? It's 9.
That's the answer!
   On this problem, have your child try it alone, and then go over
it together:

$$1 + 5 + 2 = ?$$

If your child got the correct answer, 8, review how she reached
that: First add 1 + 5 to get 6, then 6 + 2 to get 8. Then have her
do Problem Set A. If she didn't get it right, take a break and go
over this Extra Help box again when you are both ready.

Problem Set A

1. $1 + 4 + 1 =$ _____   **7.** $1 + 1 + 2 =$ _____   **13.** $6 + 2 + 1 =$ _____

2. $2 + 3 + 3 =$ _____   **8.** $4 + 3 + 1 =$ _____   **14.** $4 + 2 + 2 =$ _____

3. $2 + 1 + 1 =$ _____   **9.** $5 + 2 + 1 =$ _____   **15.** $1 + 5 + 1 =$ _____

4. $4 + 3 + 2 =$ _____   **10.** $1 + 3 + 2 =$ _____   **16.** $1 + 6 + 2 =$ _____

5. $3 + 3 + 1 =$ _____   **11.** $5 + 1 + 1 =$ _____   **17.** $5 + 3 + 1 =$ _____

6. $2 + 5 + 2 =$ _____   **12.** $3 + 1 + 3 =$ _____   **18.** $1 + 1 + 6 =$ _____

Answers on page 52.

By the end of the first grade, your child should be able to add three single-digit numbers whose sum is no more than 10, but we'll save the addition of larger numbers for the second grade. However, we do want to begin adding two single-digit numbers, whose sum is 10 or greater, so we'll work on this in the next minilesson.

But before you take your child to that next step, you need to be sure that she is ready. Math is learned sequentially, but different children learn math at different speeds. Since we're covering an entire year's work in this book, it is to be expected that you will have to repeat some of the minilessons two or three times before your child fully understands them. Be patient. The purpose is to get your child off to the right start. As a long-distance runner since high school, I can assure you that you don't start off a long race by trying to sprint. It's not how fast you go in the beginning that counts, but how far you get in the end.

MINILESSON 17

Double-Digit Sums

Double-digit numbers, like 17, 22, and 38, are numbers made up of two single-digit numbers next to each other. Until now, your child did problems with sums that were just single-digit numbers. Now he's ready to take addition one step further.

Table 3 goes up to 9 + 9. It works just like the earlier addition tables. In the upper left-hand corner there's a plus sign (+). To find the answers in this table, we need to do a box step.

Let's do 5 + 5. Start at the 5 below the plus sign and go up to the plus sign, then go to the 5 to the right of the plus sign, and then down to the number to the right of the starting number. So 5 + 5 = 10.

TABLE 3

Addition of 5 + 5 to 9 + 9

+	5	6	7	8	9
5	10	11	12	13	14
6	11	12	13	14	15
7	12	13	14	15	16
8	13	14	15	16	17
9	14	15	16	17	18

Now let's do 9 + 9. Start at the 9 in the lower left-hand corner of the table, go up to the plus sign, then across to the 9 in the upper right-hand corner, and then down to the number to the right of the starting number. We did another box step: 9 up to the plus sign, across to the 9, and then down to 18.

Now let's see if your child can do the problems in Problem Set B. Let him use the addition table if necessary.

Problem Set B

1. $7 + 7 =$ _____   7. $9 + 6 =$ _____   13. $5 + 8 =$ _____

2. $8 + 5 =$ _____   8. $8 + 7 =$ _____   14. $6 + 8 =$ _____

3. $5 + 9 =$ _____   9. $6 + 6 =$ _____   15. $6 + 7 =$ _____

4. $6 + 5 =$ _____   10. $8 + 9 =$ _____   16. $9 + 5 =$ _____

5. $8 + 8 =$ _____   11. $7 + 5 =$ _____   17. $6 + 9 =$ _____

6. $7 + 9 =$ _____   12. $9 + 9 =$ _____   18. $8 + 6 =$ _____

Answers on page 52.

If your child got each of these right, go on to the next mini-lesson. If he got only one or two wrong, help him go over them until he knows them.

If he got more than two wrong, then it may be that he needs to go back over Table 2 in Minilesson 7, then try this lesson again. Learning double-digit sums is essential because your child needs that skill to perform more advanced mathematical computations. It's just something that has to be learned first.

Another thing you can try is to make flash cards for every problem that your child has gotten wrong in each minilesson. Have him try to memorize the answers to each of these problems. You might also go over each problem using circles or boxes.

If your child still needs more help, see the Extra Help box.

EXTRA HELP

Addition

You'll need 18 coins to teach this lesson. Since addition is really a form of counting, your child will be adding various combinations of coins. Start with some easy questions.

How much is 4 + 2 ? Lay out the coins this way:

⬤ ⬤ ⬤ ⬤ + ⬤ ⬤ =

Have your child count the circles. The answer is 6.
    Then try 5 + 3:

⬤ ⬤ ⬤ ⬤ ⬤ + ⬤ ⬤ ⬤ =

The answer is 8.
    And then, 4 + 6:

⬤ ⬤ ⬤ ⬤ + ⬤ ⬤ ⬤ ⬤ ⬤ ⬤ =

The answer is 10.
    Now have your child lay out the coins. First try 4 + 4. Then
6 + 3. And then 5 + 5.
    Keep working your way up: 4 + 8; 5 + 9; 6 + 8; until you're up
to 9 + 9. Once your child seems confident, ask him to try Problem
Set C.

Problem Set C

1. 2 + 3 = _____   7. 5 + 8 = _____   13. 8 + 8 = _____

2. 3 + 4 = _____   8. 7 + 6 = _____   14. 7 + 9 = _____

3. 5 + 3 = _____   9. 6 + 9 = _____   15. 8 + 7 = _____

4. 4 + 5 = _____   10. 7 + 7 = _____   16. 9 + 6 = _____

5. 6 + 4 = _____   11. 9 + 5 = _____   17. 9 + 9 = _____

6. 4 + 7 = _____   12. 6 + 8 = _____   18. 6 + 6 = _____

Answers on page 52.

If all the answers were right, or if there is just one wrong answer, your child is ready for Minilesson 18. But more than one wrong answer indicates that more work is needed. If you and your child have the time and the inclination, do it right now. If not, it can wait until tomorrow.

When you are both ready, take out the coins again and have your child use them to do the first four or five problems in Problem Set C. Then copy all the problems over and have him do them without the coins.

It may appear that progress is slow, but each minilesson contains about a week of math, so it's fine if your child goes over each minilesson several times.

Answers to Chapter 6 Problem Sets

Problem Set A

1. 6	**6.** 9	**11.** 7	**16.** 9
2. 8	**7.** 4	**12.** 7	**17.** 9
3. 4	**8.** 8	**13.** 9	**18.** 8
4. 9	**9.** 8	**14.** 8	
5. 7	**10.** 6	**15.** 7	

Problem Set B

1. 14	**6.** 16	**11.** 12	**16.** 14
2. 13	**7.** 15	**12.** 18	**17.** 15
3. 14	**8.** 15	**13.** 13	**18.** 14
4. 11	**9.** 12	**14.** 14	
5. 16	**10.** 17	**15.** 13	

Problem Set C

1. 5	**6.** 11	**11.** 14	**16.** 15
2. 7	**7.** 13	**12.** 14	**17.** 18
3. 8	**8.** 13	**13.** 16	**18.** 12
4. 9	**9.** 15	**14.** 16	
5. 10	**10.** 14	**15.** 15	

Counting Money

So far we've occasionally used coins to help us count and do some addition and some subtraction. Now your child should be ready to tackle money problems a little more formally. In Minilesson 18 he will be working with pennies and nickels, and in Minilesson 19, with pennies, nickels, and dimes.

You'll notice that the material in each minilesson builds on the material covered in earlier minilessons. So if at any time you realize that your child needs more work with any of the problems that we covered earlier, it is extremely important to go back as far as necessary to master that material.

MINILESSON 18

Counting Pennies and Nickels

It's important that your child begin to understand the use of money—knowing how to handle it is an essential part of growing up and becoming more independent. For this lesson, you'll need 19 pennies and three nickels. Ask your child if he knows how many cents are in a penny. And how many cents there are in a nickel.

If your child knows this, then you're in business, so you can skip the rest of this paragraph. If not, lay out five pennies next to a nickel and explain that a penny is worth one cent and that there are five pennies in a nickel, so a nickel is worth 5 cents.

Place six pennies on the table and ask how much money is there. If he gets that right, then place a nickel and four pennies on the table and ask the same question. Keep making up combinations of nickels and pennies until you've worked your way up to nine pennies and two nickels. Help your child count if he gets stuck.

Now ask your child to dip into the pile of change and lay out 8 cents. Then 12 cents. Then 15 cents. Then 19 cents. It doesn't matter whether your child uses all pennies or some combination of nickels and pennies. But if your child put down 19 pennies, you can point out that it would be a lot easier to use three nickels and four pennies.

Now use the change to do addition. Ask your child, "How much is 4 cents plus 7 cents?" Use the money to figure this out. If your child got this right, go on to the next paragraph. If not, show him how to do it by taking four pennies and adding to them a nickel and two pennies.

Have your child try two more problems using the coins. First, add 8 cents and 6 cents. Next, add 9 cents and 9 cents.

Here's a set of problems for your child to solve. Ask him to add the coins together in each problem, and then to write down the answer.

Problem Set A

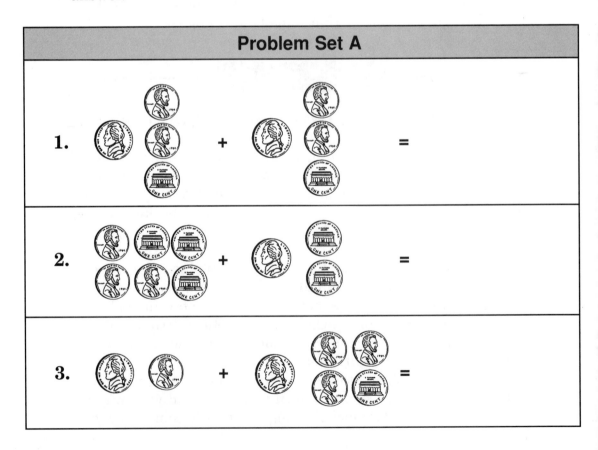

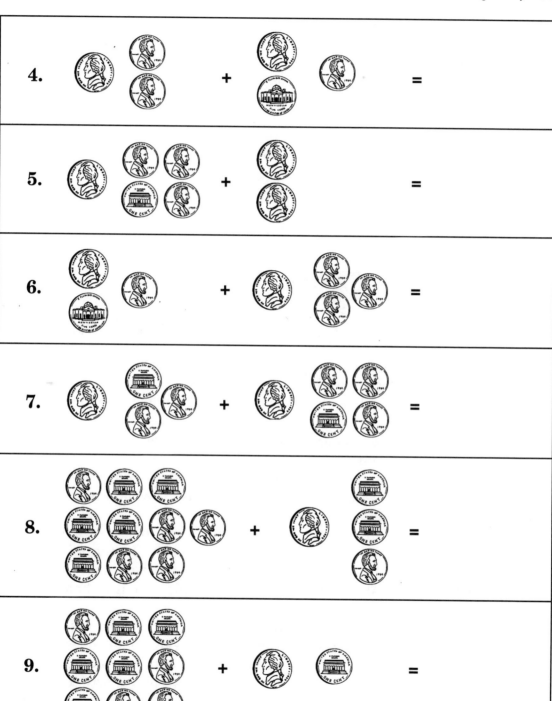

4.   +   =

5.   +   =

6.   +   =

7.   +   =

8.   +   =

9.   +   =

Answers on page 59.

If your child can use more practice, make up a few more problems. As we progress through first- and second-grade math, we'll be doing a lot more problems counting coins.

MINILESSON 19

Counting Pennies, Nickels, and Dimes

Your child has been counting just pennies and nickels until now, but in this minilesson we'll be adding dimes to the mix, so you'll need to be sure you have a dime on hand as well as three nickels and nine pennies.

First let's review some of the things we covered in the last minilesson. Ask your child how many cents there are in a nickel and in a penny. If she knows there are 5 cents in a nickel and that a penny is 1 cent, continue on. Otherwise, it would be helpful to go over Minilesson 18 again.

Place a dime in front of your child and ask her how many cents are in a dime. If she knows that there are 10 cents in a dime, then skip the rest of this paragraph. If she doesn't, then place 10 pennies alongside the dime and explain that a dime is worth 10 cents.

Now ask how many nickels make up a dime. If she knows the answer is 2, then go directly to the problem below. If she doesn't, then place five pennies next to a nickel and explain that there are five pennies, or 5 cents, in one nickel. Now, how many cents are there in two nickels?

Place three nickels in front of your child and ask how much money that is. The answer is 15 cents, or 15 pennies. Since there are five pennies in a nickel, there are 15 cents in three nickels: 5 + 5 + 5 = 15.

Next, place a dime, a nickel, and a penny in front of your child and ask how much money it is. The answer is 16 cents: 10 + 5 + 1 = 16.

Finally, place a dime, a nickel, and four pennies in front of your child and ask how much money it is. The answer is 19 cents: 10 + 5 + 4 = 19.

Problem Set B

Ask your child to add the coins together in each problem and then to write down the answer.

1. A dime plus a nickel plus two pennies = _____.

2. A dime plus eight pennies = _____.

3. One dime plus one penny plus one nickel = _____.

4. One nickel and two pennies plus one dime and two pennies = _____.

Now have your child work out these problems:

---

5. + =

---

6. + =

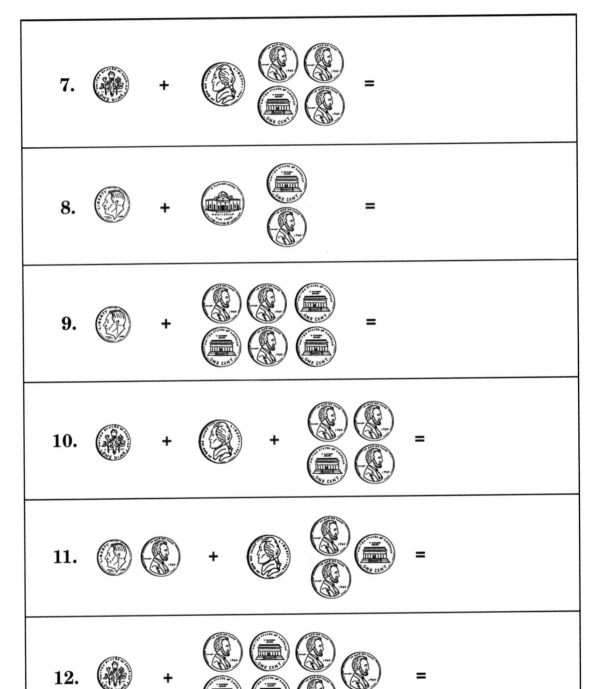

7.   +   =

8.   +   =

9.   +   =

10.   +   +   =

11.   +   =

12.   +   =

13.

Answers below.

Answers to Chapter 7 Problem Sets

Problem Set A
1. 16 cents
2. 13 cents
3. 15 cents
4. 18 cents
5. 19 cents
6. 19 cents
7. 17 cents
8. 18 cents
9. 15 cents
10. 19 cents

Problem Set B
1. 17 cents
2. 18 cents
3. 16 cents
4. 19 cents
5. 17 cents
6. 14 cents
7. 19 cents
8. 17 cents
9. 16 cents
10. 19 cents
11. 19 cents
12. 17 cents
13. 19 cents

Chapter 8

Word Problems with Single- and Double-Digit Numbers

Before your child can learn how to do word problems, she has to know that numbers can be words. The number 7, for example, can also be written as the word *seven*. And the number 4 can be written as *four*. In Minilesson 20, we'll translate words into numbers and numbers into words.

Once your child has that idea down, we'll begin to do some real word problems. In Minilesson 21, we'll be doing word problems with single-digit numbers, and in Minilesson 22, the problems will have double-digit numbers.

MINILESSON 20

Words and Numbers

First find out whether your child can write the numbers from 1 to 20 and the words that go with them.

Problem Set A

Ask your child to write the numbers that go with each of these words:

one	_____	eight	_____	fifteen	_____
two	_____	nine	_____	sixteen	_____
three	_____	ten	_____	seventeen	_____
four	_____	eleven	_____	eighteen	_____
five	_____	twelve	_____	nineteen	_____
six	_____	thirteen	_____	twenty	_____
seven	_____	fourteen	_____		

Answers on page 69.

Problem Set B

Now have her write the numbers that go with these words:

eighteen	_____	nineteen	_____	three	_____
thirteen	_____	one	_____	twenty	_____
nine	_____	zero	_____	seven	_____
seventeen	_____	twelve	_____	eleven	_____
two	_____	eight	_____		

Answers on page 69.

If your child got all of Problem Sets A and B right, then go on to the next problem set. If not, go over any numbers that she got wrong until she is sure of them.

Problem Set C

Have your child write the words that go with these numbers:

1 _____   8 _____   15 _____

2 _____   9 _____   16 _____

3 _____   10 _____   17 _____

4 _____   11 _____   18 _____

5 _____   12 _____   19 _____

6 _____   13 _____   20 _____

7 _____   14 _____

Answers on page 69.

First-graders are not the world's greatest spellers, so don't worry if your child happened to misspell a few of the numbers. As long as she knows each of these numbers, we're way ahead in the game.

MINILESSON 21

Word Problems with Single-Digit Numbers

Most students have difficulty with word problems, especially in the later grades. This is mostly because they are not used to setting up equations from words. So it would be a good idea to get your child to start thinking early of how to solve mathematical problems that are expressed in words.

Since few first-graders can read well enough to understand these problems, you will need to read them aloud to your child. If he wants to use pennies to help with these problems, that would be fine. So before you begin reading the problems, hold nine pennies in reserve. It would be great if he could do these without using the pennies, but if he is having trouble, then let him use them.

Do the following examples together.

Jason has four marbles and Lisa has five. How many marbles do they have together?

Part of the value of word problems is in learning to translate words into a numerical equation, so we set up an equation to help us find the answer. An equation is a mathematical expression with two equal sides. The numbers on either side of the equal sign are equal. Jason's four marbles plus Lisa's five marbles equals nine marbles: $4 + 5 = 9$.

Mary has eight cookies. She gives four to Boris. How many cookies does she have left?

Mary's eight cookies minus the four cookies she gives to Boris leaves her with four cookies. Again, our equation has to have two equal sides: $8 - 4 = 4$.

Before going on to Problem Set D, be sure your child understands the two examples above. He may have difficulty with this kind of problem, so be patient. It usually takes some time for a child to learn how to set up equations, which is the key to solving word problems. So read through the following word problems with your child. You may need to help him set up the equations. Once you do, though, he should be able to find the answers on his own.

Problem Set D

1. If Joseph has 2 cents and Merry has 5 cents, how much do they have altogether?

2. If a family ordered a pizza with eight slices and the parents ate three slices, how many slices are left for the children?

3. If you have a nickel and four pennies, how much money do you have?

4. If you have six nickels and you give away five, how many nickels do you have left?

5. If Sam has two videotapes, Mary has three videotapes, and Justine has one videotape, how many videotapes do they have altogether?

6. If Kristin has nine paper dolls and gives five to Karen, how many paper dolls does she have left?

7. If Joan has one marble, Eleni has four marbles, and Elizabeth has three marbles, how many marbles do they have altogether?

8. If Sam's fishbowl has four green fish, three black fish, and two goldfish, how many fish does he have in the bowl?

9. There are eight birds in the cage. Three birds are yellow. How many are not yellow?

10. Tom went into the pet shop, where he saw seven rabbits. Four rabbits were asleep. How many rabbits were awake?

11. Sally has nine cats. Four of the cats are gray. How many of the cats are not gray?

Answers on page 69.

If your child seemed to understand this, ask him to make up his own word problems. He can begin by making up a problem that's similar to the first question in Problem Set D. After he has made up a few more problems similar to those in the problem set, let him have some fun by making up more problems completely on his own. Then ask him to solve each of the problems he's made up. Check his solutions to make sure he has done them correctly.

MINILESSON 22

Word Problems with Double-Digit Numbers

So far our word problems have involved just single-digit numbers. Now we soar all the way up to the double-digit number 19.

To be sure your child is ready for this, ask her, "How much is 6 plus 5?" If she says "11," ask her, "How much is 8 plus 6?" If it took her more than 30 seconds to say that the answer is 14, she is probably having some difficulty doing this in her head. You can help by reviewing Table 3 in Minilesson 17 with her. If she was able to answer these, continue on.

Ask your child to work out this problem: Chung had seven balloons. Seth gave him eight more. How many balloons does Chung have now? The answer is 15 balloons (7 + 8 = 15).

Now let's do a subtraction problem. Kyra had 13 marbles. She gave four to Marlene. How many did she have left? The answer is 9 marbles (13 − 4 = 9).

Now have your child try Problem Set E. Remind her to set up an equation for each. If your child can read well enough, have her do these on her own. Otherwise, read each problem to her.

Problem Set E

1. How much is 7 plus 9?

2. How much is 14 minus 6?

3. Mary has 11 dolls. For Christmas she got six more. How many dolls does she have now?

4. Adam had 19 cents. He spent 12 cents. How many cents did he have left?

5. In a class of 19 students, 7 were out sick. How many were not out sick?

6. If you had a dime and a nickel, how much money would you have?

7. Jill had a dime and eight pennies. She gave 12 cents to Mike. How much money did she have left?

8. Pam has 15 dresses. Six are red. How many are not red?

9. If you had a dime, a nickel, and four pennies, how much money would you have?

10. Mark started the day with 18 cents. He gave a nickel to John and a dime to James. How much money did he have left?

11. What combinations of nickels and pennies add up to 15 cents?

Answers on page 69.

Some children are more comfortable using objects like pennies, buttons, or bottle caps to help them add and subtract. Others prefer pencil and paper. The important thing is that the child is able to set up the equation and then comes up with the right answers. As long as your child is getting these problems right, there's nothing for you to worry about.

Some children have trouble remembering the addition tables. Although they need to know all the combinations of numbers up to 9 + 9 in Table 3 in Minilesson 17, it's still fine for them to use their fingers until they are confident. In the following Extra Help box, we show how the finger method can be used for addition and subtraction. If your child definitely knows the addition tables and got each of the problems right in Problem Set E, then go directly to Chapter 9. Otherwise, review the Extra Help box with her.

EXTRA HELP

Using the Finger Method for Addition and Subtraction

Ask your child, "How much is 8 plus 6?" If she knows that 8 + 6 = 14, tell her that she can check her answer by using her fingers. If she doesn't know that 8 and 6 are 14, then explain that the finger method can help her find the answer.

Tell her to hold out both hands, palms faceup, and count off six fingers, beginning with her left thumb. Then tell her to fold down the rest of the fingers on her right hand. Now tell her to begin counting by saying "8," and then counting from her left thumb as 9 to her right pinky. She can touch each fingertip to her chin as she counts, if that helps her to keep track. When she reaches the sixth finger, she should have counted to 14.

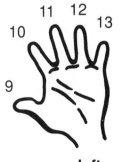 

left   right

The equation is 8 + 6 = 14.

Now we'll try another one. Ask your child, "How much is 9 plus 7?" Tell her to count off seven fingers, say, "9," and begin counting from her left thumb as 10, continuing on until she has counted seven fingers. She should reach the seventh finger as she says, "16."

The equation is 9 + 7 = 16.

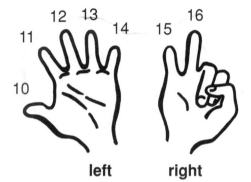

left   right

The finger method can be used in subtraction as well as addition. Ask your child, "If Khalid has 12 pennies and gives 4 to Venetia, how many pennies does he have left?"

Solution: Count off four fingers on the right hand, beginning with the right pinky. Then fold down the thumb. Now count backward for four fingers, starting with the right pinky as 11.

The equation is 12 – 4 = 8.

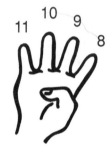

right

Now try one more: Fifteen birds were sitting on a fence. Nine flew away. How many were left?

The equation is 15 – 9 = 6.

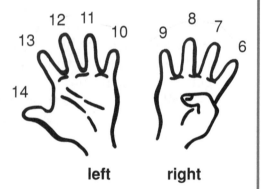

left   right

If your child can work these out in her head without using her fingers, that would be best. But there's nothing wrong with her using her fingers to figure things out. Like the training wheels on her bicycle, the finger method can be discarded when she's confident that she can get along without it.

Answers to Chapter 8 Problem Sets

Problem Set A

one	1	eight	8	fifteen	15
two	2	nine	9	sixteen	16
three	3	ten	10	seventeen	17
four	4	eleven	11	eighteen	18
five	5	twelve	12	nineteen	19
six	6	thirteen	13	twenty	20
seven	7	fourteen	14		

Problem Set B

eighteen	18	nineteen	19	three	3
thirteen	13	one	1	twenty	20
nine	9	zero	0	seven	7
seventeen	17	twelve	12	eleven	11
two	2	eight	8		

Problem Set C

1	one	8	eight	15	fifteen
2	two	9	nine	16	sixteen
3	three	10	ten	17	seventeen
4	four	11	eleven	18	eighteen
5	five	12	twelve	19	nineteen
6	six	13	thirteen	20	twenty
7	seven	14	fourteen		

Problem Set D

1. 7 cents $(2 + 5 = 7)$
2. five slices $(8 - 3 = 5)$
3. 9 cents $(5 + 4 = 9)$
4. one nickel $(6 - 5 = 1)$
5. six videotapes $(2 + 3 + 1 = 6)$
6. four paper dolls $(9 - 5 = 4)$
7. eight marbles $(1 + 4 + 3 = 8)$
8. nine fish $(4 + 3 + 2 = 9)$
9. five birds $(8 - 3 = 5)$
10. three rabbits $(7 - 4 = 3)$
11. five cats $(9 - 4 = 5)$

Problem Set E

1. 16 $(7 + 9 = 16)$
2. 8 $(14 - 6 = 8)$
3. 17 dolls $(11 + 6 = 17)$
4. 7 cents $(19 - 12 = 7)$
5. 12 students $(19 - 7 = 12)$
6. 15 cents $(10 + 5 = 15)$
7. 6 cents $(10 + 8 = 18; 18 - 12 = 6)$
8. nine dresses $(15 - 6 = 9)$
9. 19 cents $(10 + 5 + 4 = 19)$
10. 3 cents $(18 - 5 = 13; 13 - 10 = 3)$
11. There are four combinations:
   1. 15 pennies
   2. 10 pennies and one nickel
   3. five pennies and two nickels
   4. three nickels

Chapter 9

Introduction to Telling Time

During the first grade your child should begin learning to tell time. This chapter will get him started. Minilesson 23 will introduce conventional (or round-faced) clocks, and Minilesson 24 will introduce digital clocks.

MINILESSON 23

Telling Time on Conventional Clocks

When I was four years old, my mother asked me what time it was, knowing, of course, that I couldn't tell time. But I went into the kitchen and looked at the clock. I told my mother, "I can't read the numbers, but the hands of the clock look like this." And I stretched out my arms as far as I could. Now to this day I don't know if it was a quarter past nine or a quarter to three.

For the first grade we'll work only on telling time on the hour and the half hour, and leave the more detailed concepts to the beginning of the second grade.

Explain to your child that the shorter hand of the clock is the hour hand. When the hour hand points to the five, which it does on the clock below, it is five o'clock, which can also be written as 5:00. When it is exactly five o'clock, the minute hand, which is the longer hand, will be pointing to the 12.

Then explain that when the minute hand is pointing to the 6, it is half past the hour. For example, on the clock to the right, it is half past five, or 5:30. Explain that when it is 5:30, the hour hand is halfway between 5 and 6. And when it is 8:30, the hour hand is halfway between 8 and 9.

Can your child tell time? Find out by asking him what time it is on each of these clocks:

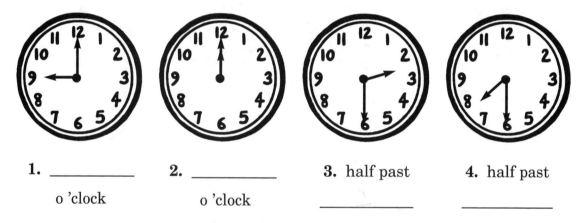

1. _____
   o 'clock

2. _____
   o 'clock

3. half past
   _____

4. half past
   _____

Answers: 1. nine o'clock; 2. twelve o'clock; 3. half past two; 4. half past seven

The answer to the third question, half past two, can also be expressed as 2:30, or two thirty. Also, the answer to the fourth question, half past seven, can be expressed as 7:30, or seven thirty.

Now ask your child to figure out what time it is on each of these clocks:

5. three   6. eight   7. ten   8. four

Answers: 5. three o'clock, or 3:00; 6. eight o'clock, or 8:00; 7. half past ten, or 10:30, or ten thirty; 8. half past three, or 3:30, or three thirty

Ask your child to set each clock for the times shown under each clock:

9. four o'clock   **10.** ten o'clock   **11.** nine thirty   **12.** two thirty

Answers:

MINILESSON 24

Telling Time on Digital Clocks

Since so many clocks are digital these days, your child needs to learn how to tell time using digital clocks, too. Ask her to read the times on these clocks:

This is read as "four o'clock."

This is read as "half past eight," or "eight thirty."

Next, have your child write down what time it is on each of these clocks:

1. _____ 2. _____ 3. _____

4. _____ 5. _____ 6. _____

Answers: 1. three thirty, or half past three; 2. twelve o'clock; 3. one o'clock; 4. eleven thirty, or half past eleven; 5. two thirty, or half past two; 6. seven o'clock

Ask your child what time it is on each of these clocks:

7. _____ 8. _____ 9. _____

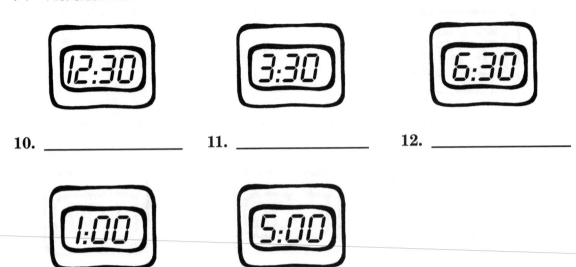

10. _____   11. _____   12. _____

13. _____   14. _____

Answers: 7. half past four, or four thirty; 8. eight o'clock; 9. eleven o'clock; 10. half past twelve, or twelve thirty; 11. half past three, or three thirty; 12. half past six, or six thirty; 13. one o'clock; 14. five o'clock

Chapter 10

Double-Digit Addition and Subtraction

This chapter covers adding and subtracting double-digit numbers. Minilessons 25 and 26 cover addition, and Minilesson 27 covers subtraction. Adding double-digit numbers is easy as long as you don't have to carry. Likewise, double-digit subtraction is easy as long as you don't have to borrow. Your child doesn't have to worry about carrying and borrowing until second-grade math.

MINILESSON 25

Double-Digit Addition: Part 1

Once your child has gotten good at adding two and three single-digit numbers, she can try adding two double-digit numbers. Can your child add 21 and 36 in her head? Probably not, unless she is a math prodigy. Indeed, it would take most adults more than 10 or even 15 seconds to add two double-digit numbers without using pencil and paper.

But ask your child to work out the same problem when it's presented like this:

$$\begin{array}{r} 21 \\ +36 \\ \hline \end{array}$$

If your child got 57, go on to the next problem. If not, explain it step by step: Ask her, "How much is 1 plus 6?" Show her where to write the 7. And then ask, "How much is two 10s + three 10s?" Show her where to write the five 10s. Now read the number: 57.

Next problem:

$$22$$
$$\underline{+14}$$

If your child answered 36, then have her do Problem Set A. If not, you'll need to explain it step by step. Ask, "How much is 2 plus 4?" Have your child write the answer. And then, "How much is two 10s plus one 10?" Have her write the answer. And then ask your child to read the answer, 36.

Adding double-digit numbers takes exactly the same skills as adding single-digit numbers. But you need to make certain that your child has a firm foundation in adding single digits. Mathematics is based on developing basic skills and building on them to do more advanced work. You cannot add double-digit numbers unless you know the addition table or can at least count on your fingers. So if your child is having problems here or is at all uncertain about adding single-digit numbers, please turn back to Table 1 in Minilesson 6 and go through it until she can do every single addition problem correctly in that table. Learning math is a lot like learning to dance. Sometimes you need to take one step back before you can take two steps forward. There's nothing wrong with that. The important point is to get wherever it is that you're going.

Problem Set A

1. 71	**2.** 30	**3.** 35	**4.** 21	**5.** 10	**6.** 77
+26	+24	+64	+67	+33	+11

7. 14	**8.** 20	**9.** 62	**10.** 23	**11.** 47	**12.** 17
+63	+60	+17	+55	+20	+12

13. 11 +68	**14.** 13 +46	**15.** 61 +21	**16.** 16 +42	**17.** 72 +12	**18.** 10 +56
19. 18 +31	**20.** 84 +13	**21.** 59 +30	**22.** 44 +41	**23.** 66 +22	**24.** 34 +15

Answers on page 83.

If your child got all the problems right in this minilesson, the next one can be skipped. But if she got one or two wrong, then she can use some more practice. She definitely needs to complete Minilesson 26.

MINILESSON 26

Double-Digit Addition: Part 2

If your child got through Problem Set A with few mistakes, let's see how he does with the Problem Set B. If, after these problems are completed, you feel that your child definitely has no difficulty adding single-digit numbers and using that knowledge to add double-digit numbers, then go on to the next minilesson. If not, then turn back to Minilesson 6.

Here's another problem set for your child to work out.

Problem Set B

1. 14
+35

2. 17
+42

3. 36
+42

4. 15
+13

5. 84
+13

6. 62
+26

7. 43
+26

8. 57
+31

9. 21
+47

10. 64
+24

11. 83
+13

12. 55
+42

13. 33
+66

14. 75
+14

15. 38
+41

16. 15
+32

17. 61
+24

18. 73
+16

19. 53
+46

20. 66
+12

21. 24
+43

22. 48
+11

23. 31
+54

24. 82
+17

Answers on page 83.

MINILESSON 27

Double-Digit Subtraction

Subtracting double-digit numbers is virtually the same as subtracting single-digit numbers, except that you get to do it twice. Tell your child that it's like getting two prizes in a box of Cracker Jack.

Have your child try this problem:

$$74$$
$$-32$$

If she wrote 42, then go on to the next problem. If not, then ask, "How much is 4 take away 2?" And, "How much is seven 10s take away three 10s?" Show her how to write the answer.

Now ask her to try this problem:

$$35$$
$$-23$$

Here we have $5 - 3 = 2$ and three 10s − two 10s = one 10, or 30 take away 20 equals 10. So the answer is 12.

Now have your child try these problems:

56	89	97
−32	−25	−16

If she got 24, 64, and 81, then it's time to go on to the problem sets that follow. But if all three answers were wrong, then you should review Minilessons 8, 9, and 10, which deal with subtracting single-digit numbers. If only one or two answers were wrong, then let's see how she does on Problem Sets C, D, and E.

Problem Set C

1. 45	**2.** 56	**3.** 69	**4.** 67	**5.** 97	**6.** 80
−24	−45	−16	−34	−14	−50

7. 83
−53

8. 66
−25

9. 77
−55

10. 89
−34

11. 17
−10

12. 94
−14

Answers on page 83.

If your child does Problem Set D correctly, you can skip Problem Set E and go directly to the next chapter. But if she is having some difficulty, have her do Problem Set E as well.

Problem Set D

1. 88
−44

2. 96
−35

3. 43
−21

4. 75
−53

5. 82
−21

6. 38
−15

7. 47
−25

8. 55
−34

9. 29
−12

10. 68
−45

11. 34
−13

12. 79
−61

13. 58
−23

14. 27
−11

15. 49
−36

16. 95
−71

17. 84
−72

18. 62
−21

Answers on page 83.

Problem Set E

1. 66 −41	**2.** 75 −63	**3.** 47 −34	**4.** 92 −30	**5.** 86 −35	**6.** 43 −22
7. 55 −43	**8.** 69 −57	**9.** 38 −14	**10.** 24 −20	**11.** 76 −51	**12.** 89 −24
13. 98 −36	**14.** 44 −21	**15.** 87 −22	**16.** 90 −70	**17.** 66 −55	**18.** 71 −10

Answers on page 83.

Before going any further, you must be certain that your child can add and subtract. If your child is still not confident about adding and subtracting, then go over the following Extra Help box with your child. See if your child can work through the entire box.

Addition and Subtraction Using the Number Line

First let's try the following addition problem using the number line next to it:

6 + 7 = _____

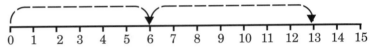

Count up six spaces on the line and then add seven more spaces to that. Where do you end up? You should end up at 13.

   Next problem:

4 + 8 = _____

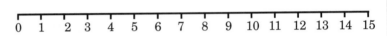

Did you end up with 12? You go four spaces and then another eight, which gives you a total of 12.

   Last addition problem: Draw your own number line in the space below and figure out:

5 + 9 = _____

Here's the solution:

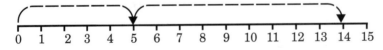 $5 + 9 = 14$

   Now we'll do some subtraction. Use the number line below to find the answer to the problem:

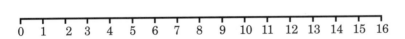   15 − 7 = _____

Was your answer 8? Here's how I did it:

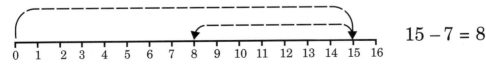 $15 - 7 = 8$

One more subtraction problem and we're finished. Find the answer to 17 − 5, drawing your own number line in the space below.

Did you get 12? I've worked it out here:

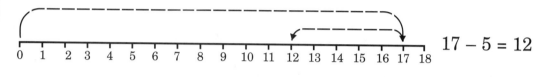

$17 - 5 = 12$

Answers to Chapter 10 Problem Sets

Problem Set A

1. 97	**2.** 54	**3.** 99	**4.** 88	**5.** 43	**6.** 88
7. 77	**8.** 80	**9.** 79	**10.** 78	**11.** 67	**12.** 29
13. 79	**14.** 59	**15.** 82	**16.** 58	**17.** 84	**18.** 66
19. 49	**20.** 97	**21.** 89	**22.** 85	**23.** 88	**24.** 49

Problem Set B

1. 49	**2.** 59	**3.** 78	**4.** 28	**5.** 97	**6.** 88
7. 69	**8.** 88	**9.** 68	**10.** 88	**11.** 96	**12.** 97
13. 99	**14.** 89	**15.** 79	**16.** 47	**17.** 85	**18.** 89
19. 99	**20.** 78	**21.** 67	**22.** 59	**23.** 85	**24.** 99

Problem Set C

1. 21	**2.** 11	**3.** 53	**4.** 33	**5.** 83	**6.** 30
7. 30	**8.** 41	**9.** 22	**10.** 55	**11.** 7	**12.** 80

Problem Set D

1. 44	**2.** 61	**3.** 22	**4.** 22	**5.** 61	**6.** 23
7. 22	**8.** 21	**9.** 17	**10.** 23	**11.** 21	**12.** 18
13. 35	**14.** 16	**15.** 13	**16.** 24	**17.** 12	**18.** 41

Problem Set E

1. 25	**2.** 12	**3.** 13	**4.** 62	**5.** 51	**6.** 21
7. 12	**8.** 12	**9.** 24	**10.** 4	**11.** 15	**12.** 65
13. 62	**14.** 23	**15.** 65	**16.** 20	**17.** 11	**18.** 61

Word Problems with and without Money

In Minilesson 28 we'll do word problems without money, and in Minilesson 29 we'll do word problems with money. In both mini-lessons your child will be reinforcing his learning in how to set up equations from words and do double-digit subtraction.

MINILESSON 28

Word Problems without Money

Read each of these problems to your child. If he can solve them in his head, that's excellent. But part of the value of these word problems is in learning how to translate the words into a numerical equation, so have him write the equation and the answer for each.

Problem Set A

1. How much is 7 minus 4?

2. If Bill had nine marbles and gave four of them to Martha, how many would he have left?

3. How much is 8 minus 2?

4. If nine people were riding on a bus and three got off, how many people would still be on the bus?

5. If Jason cut his birthday cake into eight slices and gave a slice to each of his six friends, how many slices would be left for him to eat?

6. How much is 26 take away 12?

7. How much is 78 minus 12?

8. If 98 quarts of milk were delivered to a grocery store in the morning, and there were 11 quarts left at closing time, how many quarts were sold during that day?

9. How much is 66 minus 43?

10. How much is 94 take away 72?

11. If Mark had 29 comic books and gave 14 of them to his friends, how many would he have left?

12. If Paul baked 88 cookies, ate 12 of them, and gave the rest away, how many cookies did he give away?

Answers on page 88.

If your child set up each equation correctly and got the right answer for each, go directly to the next minilesson. If he needs extra help doing word problems without money, go over the Extra Help box with him.

Word Problems without Money

Let's use two questions from Problem Set A as examples of how word problems should be done. Here's the first: How much is 26 take away 12? Another way of writing this problem is:

$$26$$
$$\underline{-12}$$

And from there, all we need to do is subtract the 2 from the 6, and then subtract the one 10 from the two 10s.

Now let's try a second problem: If 98 quarts of milk were delivered to a grocery store in the morning, and there were 11 quarts left at closing time, how many quarts were sold during that day?

$$98$$
$$\underline{-11}$$

To solve this problem, we just subtract:

$$98$$
$$\underline{-11}$$
$$87$$

Tell your child that when he sees a word problem, he should first set up the equation rather than try to solve it in his head. Not that there's anything wrong with being able to solve it in his head, but he can cut down on mistakes by first setting up the equation.

MINILESSON 29

Word Problems with Money

So far your child has learned how to handle word problems, double-digit subtraction, and money problems. Now let's combine all three types of problems.

Here's an example: You have 36 cents and give your friend two dimes. How much do you have left? If your child can do this correctly in her head, that's great, but she should still set up the equation. Her answer should look like this:

$$\begin{array}{r} 10 \\ +10 \\ \hline 20 \text{ cents} \end{array} \qquad \begin{array}{r} 36 \\ -20 \\ \hline 16 \text{ cents} \end{array}$$

If she had trouble with this, count out three dimes and six pennies. Then take away two dimes. What's left? Your child should be able to count one dime and six pennies, which equals 16 cents.

Now try this one: Joseph has 84 cents. He gives a dime to Jerry and two pennies to Sue. How much does he have left?

Solution:

$$\begin{array}{r} 10 \\ +\ 2 \\ \hline 12 \end{array} \qquad \begin{array}{r} 84 \\ -12 \\ \hline 72 \text{ cents} \end{array}$$

Problem Set B

1. If you start the day with 75 cents and spend 22 cents, how much money do you have left?

2. How much is 83 cents minus 32 cents?

3. If you started with four dimes and eight pennies and ended up with one dime and two pennies, how much money did you spend?

4. Kelly had seven dimes and a nickel. If she spent 21 cents, how much money did she have left?

5. Mike gave Marsha and Jennifer each a nickel. If he had two dimes and a nickel left, how much money did he have to begin with?

6. Kyra began the day with 89 cents. She gave a dime
to Sue Ann and a nickel to Alan. How much money
did she have left?

Answers below.

Answers to Chapter 11 Problem Sets

Problem Set A

1.
$$\begin{array}{r} 7 \\ \underline{-4} \\ 3 \end{array}$$

2.
$$\begin{array}{r} 9 \\ \underline{-4} \\ 5 \text{ marbles} \end{array}$$

3.
$$\begin{array}{r} 8 \\ \underline{-2} \\ 6 \end{array}$$

4.
$$\begin{array}{r} 9 \\ \underline{-3} \\ 6 \text{ people} \end{array}$$

5.
$$\begin{array}{r} 8 \\ \underline{6} \\ 2 \text{ slices} \end{array}$$

6.
$$\begin{array}{r} 26 \\ \underline{-12} \\ 14 \end{array}$$

7.
$$\begin{array}{r} 78 \\ \underline{-12} \\ 66 \end{array}$$

8.
$$\begin{array}{r} 98 \\ \underline{-11} \\ 87 \text{ quarts} \end{array}$$

9.
$$\begin{array}{r} 66 \\ \underline{-43} \\ 23 \end{array}$$

10.
$$\begin{array}{r} 94 \\ \underline{-72} \\ 22 \end{array}$$

11.
$$\begin{array}{r} 29 \\ \underline{-14} \\ 15 \text{ comic books} \end{array}$$

12.
$$\begin{array}{r} 88 \\ \underline{-12} \\ 76 \text{ cookies} \end{array}$$

Problem Set B

1.
$$\begin{array}{r} 75 \\ \underline{-22} \\ 53 \text{ cents} \end{array}$$

2.
$$\begin{array}{r} 83 \\ \underline{-32} \\ 51 \text{ cents} \end{array}$$

3.
$$\begin{array}{r} 10 \\ +10 \\ +10 \\ +10 \\ +\ 8 \\ \hline 48 \end{array}$$
$$\begin{array}{r} 10 \\ \underline{+2} \\ 12 \end{array}$$
$$\begin{array}{r} 48 \\ \underline{-12} \\ 36 \text{ cents} \end{array}$$

4.
$$\begin{array}{r} 10 \\ +10 \\ +10 \\ +10 \\ +10 \\ +10 \\ +10 \\ +\ 5 \\ \hline 75 \end{array}$$
$$\begin{array}{r} 75 \\ \underline{-21} \\ 54 \text{ cents} \end{array}$$

5.
$$\begin{array}{r} 5 \\ \underline{+5} \\ 10 \end{array}$$
$$\begin{array}{r} 10 \\ +10 \\ +\ 5 \\ \hline 25 \end{array}$$
$$\begin{array}{r} 25 \\ \underline{+10} \\ 35 \text{ cents} \end{array}$$

6.
$$\begin{array}{r} 10 \\ +\ 5 \\ \hline 15 \end{array}$$
$$\begin{array}{r} 89 \\ \underline{-15} \\ 74 \end{array}$$

Chapter 12

Counting Pennies, Nickels, and Dimes

In Minilessons 30 and 31 your child will learn to count money, first using straightforward addition of single- and double-digit numbers, and then by converting word problems into addition problems.

Counting Money: Part 1

As a brief money review, ask your child these questions: A penny is how many cents? How many cents in a nickel? In a dime? If she remembers that a penny is 1 cent and that there are 5 cents in a nickel and 10 cents in a dime, then continue on. If she doesn't remember, then review Minilesson 19.

Now see if your child can figure this one out in her head:

If you have two dimes and a nickel, how much money is that altogether?

Solution:

$$\begin{array}{r} 10 \\ +10 \\ \underline{+\ 5} \\ 25 \text{ cents} \end{array}$$

Your child may already know that 25 cents make a quarter. But until the second grade, when she learns how to carry, we will work with just pennies, nickels, and dimes.

To answer the next question, she can use pencil and paper.

How much is a dime, a nickel, and a penny?

Solution:

$$
\begin{array}{r}
10 \\
+ \ 5 \\
+ \ 1 \\
\hline
16 \text{ cents}
\end{array}
$$

One more question:

How much is four dimes, a nickel, and two pennies?

Solution:

$$
\begin{array}{r}
10 \\
+10 \\
+10 \\
+10 \\
+ \ 5 \\
+ \ 2 \\
\hline
47 \text{ cents}
\end{array}
$$

That last problem was a hard one. If your child got this one right, she really knows her money. If she didn't, there's nothing to worry about, because money problems this hard are usually not covered until the second grade.

Let's try a few coin tricks that will help your child become more comfortable with money. Here's the first one:

If you had just dimes and pennies, how many dimes and how many pennies would you use to count out 36 cents in change? Use the fewest coins possible.

In 36 cents there are _____ dimes and

_____ pennies.

Answer: three dimes and six pennies

Here's another one: How many dimes and pennies would you use to make 84 cents?

In 84 cents there are _____ dimes and

_____ pennies.

Answer: eight dimes and four pennies.

One more question:

In 13 cents there are _____ dime(s) and

_____ pennies.

Answer: one dime and three pennies

How much money is four dimes? How much money is two dimes?

Answers: Four dimes are 40 cents. Two dimes are 20 cents.

I'm sure that you and your child have seen better coin tricks than the ones we just did. We're just trying to get her used to using dimes and pennies. Now let's see how she does with Problem Set A.

Problem Set A

1. How many dimes and pennies would you use to make 88 cents?

2. Five dimes make _____ cents.

3. How many dimes and pennies would you use to make 68 cents?

4. If you had 52 cents in dimes and pennies, how many dimes and pennies would you have?

5. Nine dimes make _____ cents.

6. How many dimes and pennies would you use to make 95 cents?

Answers on page 95.

Before you even check your child's answers, have her go directly to Problem Set B.

Problem Set B

1. If you had a dime, a nickel, and four pennies, how much money would you have altogether?

2. How much is two pennies and three dimes?

3. If you had four dimes, a nickel, and three pennies, how much money would you have?

4. How much is two dimes, a nickel, and three pennies?

5. What is the sum of six dimes, a nickel, and two pennies?

6. If you had nine dimes and two pennies, how much money would you have?

Answers on page 95.

If your child got no more than one wrong in either problem set, go directly to Minilesson 31. If she got two or more wrong in either set, place a pile of change on the table and make up your own problems. Then have your child make up her own problems.

MINILESSON 31

Counting Money: Part 2

We know that there are 5 cents in a nickel and 10 cents in a dime. Put a pile of change in front of your child and ask him to come up with 23 cents using the fewest possible coins.

If he used two dimes and three pennies, go directly to the next problem. If he used nickels and pennies, explain that it's easier to use dimes than nickels, although four nickels and three pennies do add up to 23 cents. Of course, 23 pennies also add up to 23 cents, but we can save a lot of time by using dimes rather than pennies.

Now try these problems:

Find 36 cents using just five coins.
Solution: Three dimes, a nickel, and a penny

Find 47 cents, using the fewest possible coins.
Solution: Four dimes, a nickel, and two pennies

How much money is shown here?

           Answer: 15 cents

How much money is shown here?

              Answer: 37 cents

If your child can do those problems, he probably can do Problem Set C.

Problem Set C

For each of these, write down the amount of money shown:

1.

2.

3.

4.

5.

6.

Using the fewest possible coins, find:

7. 39 cents

8. 46 cents

9. 42 cents

Answers below.

Answers to Chapter 12 Problem Sets

Problem Set A
1. eight dimes and eight pennies
2. 50
3. six dimes and eight pennies
4. five dimes and two pennies
5. 90
6. nine dimes and five pennies

Problem Set B

1.
```
  10
 + 5
 + 4
 19 cents
```

2.
```
   2
 +10
 +10
 +10
 32 cents
```

3.
```
  10
 +10
 +10
 +10
 + 5
 + 3
 48 cents
```

4.
```
  10
 +10
 + 5
 + 3
 28 cents
```

5.
```
  10
 +10
 +10
 +10
 +10
 +10
 + 5
 + 2
 67 cents
```

6.
```
  10
 +10
 +10
 +10
 +10
 +10
 +10
 +10
 +10
 + 2
 92 cents
```

Problem Set C
1. 42 cents
2. 46 cents
3. 63 cents
4. 59 cents
5. 39 cents
6. 88 cents
7. three dimes, one nickel, four pennies
8. four dimes, one nickel, one penny
9. four dimes, two pennies

Chapter 13

Ordinal Numbers

Ordinal numbers are used to rank things. Here are two examples: Wei Tan placed *third* among Westinghouse Scholarship winners. Christmas is on the *25th* of December. Ordinal numbers have a limited usefulness in later mathematics, but your child should understand what they are by the end of the first grade. Minilessons 32, 33, and 34 will thoroughly familiarize your child with ordinal numbers. Then in Minilesson 35, her knowledge of ordinal numbers will be used to read a calendar.

MINILESSON 32

Ordinal Numbers: Part 1

In mathematics, cardinal numbers (e.g., 1, 2, 3, and 4) are used almost exclusively. But every so often problems are stated in terms of ordinal numbers, such as first, second, third, and fourth.

To see if your child is familiar with ordinal numbers, ask her to draw the third figure from this row (going from left to right) in the space to the right.

Did she draw the circle? Right or wrong, now ask her to draw these figures from the row in the space below:

the fourth figure   the second figure   the first figure

How did she do? If she got everything right, then you can go on to the next paragraph. If not, explain that when there are four objects in a line, we call them out in order from left to right. Pointing to each object, show her the first, the second, the third, and the fourth. Then ask your child to point to each in turn and call them out as you just did.

Now ask your child, "Which is the first letter of the alphabet?" And, "Which is the second?"

Now have her answer each of the questions below.

1. The third letter of the alphabet is _____.

2. The fifth letter of the alphabet is _____.

3. The fourth letter of the alphabet is _____.

4. The sixth letter of the alphabet is _____.

5. The second letter of the alphabet is _____.

Answers:

1. C   **2.** E   **3.** D   **4.** F   **5.** B

Now have her try this set of questions. If she can write the answers—either in words (e.g., first, second, third) or numbers (1st, 2nd, 3rd)—that would be best. If she can't do this, try reading the questions aloud and have your child tell you her answers. Then practice the written forms with her before continuing.

1. D is the _____ letter of the alphabet.

2. F is the _____ letter of the alphabet.

3. A is the _____ letter of the alphabet.

4. E is the _____ letter of the alphabet.

5. C is the _____ letter of the alphabet.

Answers:

1. fourth, or 4th   **2.** sixth, or 6th   **3.** first, or 1st
4. fifth, or 5th   **5.** third, or 3rd

If your child got all these right, go on to Problem Set A. If not, repeat the lesson before trying the problem set.

Problem Set A

1. B is the _____ letter of the alphabet.

2. G is the _____ letter of the alphabet.

3. The eighth letter of the alphabet is _____.

4. The fifth letter of the alphabet is _____.

5. Here is a set of numbers: 2, 5, 6, 8, 12, 15. The third number is _____.

6. Here is a set of numbers: 14, 19, 22, 29, 31, 38. The fifth number is _____.

Answers on page 104.

MINILESSON 33

Ordinal Numbers: Part 2

Ordinal numbers give us the order of a group of objects, but they don't tell us how many there are in total. Ask your child to circle the third number shown below, and then to circle the fifth number.

6   2   4   8   3   9   2

If he circled the right numbers, then skip the rest of this paragraph. If not, review the ordinal numbers and what they mean. Point to the first, second, third, fourth, fifth, sixth, and seventh numbers on the list above, saying each ordinal number aloud. Then ask your child to point to each number and say which is the first, second, third, fourth, fifth, sixth, and seventh.

Using the picture below, ask your child to draw the fifth and seventh objects in the space provided.

○ □ ◇ ⌓ △ | ▭

If he got these right, go on to the next paragraph. But if he got either wrong, ask him to point to each object and tell you which is first, second, third, fourth, fifth, sixth, and seventh.

Now ask your child to write the ordinal numbers from first to tenth as words—first, second, third—and then as numbers—1st, 2nd, 3rd. Have him continue this list:

first _____   _____

second _____   _____

_____   _____

_____   _____

_____   _____

Answers: first, second, third, fourth, fifth, sixth, seventh, eighth, ninth, tenth

(Does spelling count? Not in this book. We're happy just to get the math right.)

Now ask him to continue this list of ordinal numbers:

1st _____   _____

2nd _____   _____

_____   _____

_____   _____

_____   _____

Answers: 1st, 2nd, 3rd, 4th, 5th, 6th, 7th, 8th, 9th, 10th

If your child got these right, then he's gone beyond what he really needs to know at this point. Most children get several wrong, and that's mainly because their writing skills have not developed enough to deal with ordinal numbers this way. It's nothing to worry about until at least the third or fourth grade. The next two problem sets are a lot easier.

Problem Set B

Have your child answer these questions about this line of ten lunch boxes.

1. Whose lunch box is eighth?   _____

2. Whose lunch box is second?   _____

3. Whose lunch box is tenth?   _____

4. Whose lunch box is fourth?   _____

5. Whose lunch box is seventh?   _____

6. Whose lunch box is first?   _____

7. Whose lunch box is sixth?   _____

8. Whose lunch box is third?   _____

9. Whose lunch box is fifth?   _____

10. Whose lunch box is ninth?   _____

Answers on page 104.

Problem Set C

1. C is the _____ letter of the alphabet.
2. H is the _____ letter of the alphabet.
3. F is the _____ letter of the alphabet.
4. D is the _____ letter of the alphabet.
5. I is the _____ letter of the alphabet.
6. E is the _____ letter of the alphabet.
7. J is the _____ letter of the alphabet.

Answers on page 104.

Problem Set D

1. The fourth letter of the alphabet is _____.
2. The seventh letter of the alphabet is _____.
3. The fifth letter of the alphabet is _____.
4. The ninth letter of the alphabet is _____.
5. The sixth letter of the alphabet is _____.
6. The tenth letter of the alphabet is _____.
7. The third letter of the alphabet is _____.

Answers on page 104.

Ordinal Numbers: Part Three

So far we've done ordinal numbers ranging from first through 10th. Now we'll be going up to 31st. That will enable your child to read a calendar.

Your child does not have to know how to write the words for ordinal numbers, because several of them are rather hard to spell for a first-grader—numbers like eleventh, fifteenth, and nineteenth. Instead, point to each number and ask her to say each aloud as an ordinal number.

Cover the right column with an index card and move it down as your child states each ordinal number.

1	first, or 1st	16	sixteenth, or 16th
2	second, or 2nd	17	seventeenth, or 17th
3	third, or 3rd	18	eighteenth, or 18th
4	fourth, or 4th	19	nineteenth, or 19th
5	fifth, or 5th	20	twentieth, or 20th
6	sixth, or 6th	21	twenty-first, or 21st
7	seventh, or 7th	22	twenty-second, or 22nd
8	eighth, or 8th	23	twenty-third, or 23rd
9	ninth, or 9th	24	twenty-fourth, or 24th
10	tenth, or 10th	25	twenty-fifth, or 25th
11	eleventh, or 11th	26	twenty-sixth, or 26th
12	twelfth, or 12th	27	twenty-seventh, or 27th
13	thirteenth, or 13th	28	twenty-eighth, or 28th
14	fourteenth, or 14th	29	twenty-ninth, or 29th
15	fifteenth, or 15th	30	thirtieth, or 30th
		31	thirty-first, or 31st

Did your child miss a few? Well, that's nothing to worry about, because ordinal numbers, while useful, are not mathematical building blocks. They can be helpful, but it's not essential for your child to fully understand them in the first grade in order to progress in math.

MINILESSON 35

Reading a Calendar

By the end of the first grade, your child should be able to easily recognize all the numbers on a calendar. He should also learn when pointing to a particular day of the month that it is the 3rd, or the 12th, or the 22nd. So what you might do is point to each number, in order, and ask your child what the date is. For example, in May, your child would start with May first and go all the way up through May 31st.

Using a calendar, point to today's date and ask your child what ordinal number it is. Then, since children are always interested in their birthdays, have your child find his birthday on the calendar. You may need to help with finding the month, depending on his reading skills. Then ask him to find Halloween and New Year's Eve as well. Explain that both holidays are on the 31st day of the 10th and 12th months.

You can also show your child the number of days in a week and the number of days in a month. And then the number of weeks in a month.

Using the calendar that follows, ask your child to name the days of the week, beginning with Sunday. Ask in ordinal terms: "What is the first day of the week?" "What is the second day of the week?" And so on, through the seventh day of the week.

This may seem like a reading test, but it reinforces your child's knowledge of ordinal numbers. After your child does the days, he's ready for more questions about dates of the month.

June						
Sunday	Monday	Tuesday	Wednesday	Thursday	Friday	Saturday
			1	2	3	4
⑤	6	7	8	9	10	11
12	13	⑭	15	16	⑰	18
19	⑳	21	22	23	24	25
㉖	27	28	29	㉚		

Can your child name each of the circled dates as ordinal numbers? See if he can write them down. But if he can state them, that would certainly be good enough.

Answers: fifth, or 5th; fourteenth, or 14th; seventeenth, or 17th; twentieth, or 20th; twenty-sixth, or 26th; thirtieth, or 30th

Answers to Chapter 13 Problem Sets

Problem Set A
1. second
2. seventh
3. H
4. E
5. 6
6. 31

Problem Set B
1. Max's
2. Bill's
3. Beth's
4. John's
5. Karen's
6. Sue's
7. Jason's
8. Mary's
9. Ted's
10. Mel's

Problem Set C
1. third
2. eighth
3. sixth
4. fourth
5. ninth
6. fifth
7. tenth

Problem Set D
1. D
2. G
3. E
4. I
5. F
6. J
7. C

Chapter 14

Introduction to Fractions

In Minilessons 36 and 37, your child will learn about halves, thirds, and quarters by identifying these fractions and by dividing various geometric figures into those fractions as well. The main purpose of these minilessons is to introduce fractions and make them familiar to the child, so that he will have an easier time working with them in higher grades.

MINILESSON 36

Fractions: Part 1

The dictionary defines a fraction as one of a few (or several) equal parts of a whole. In the first grade, the fractions of ½, ⅓, and ¼ are introduced.

A good way of explaining fractions is by dividing food, clay, paper, or other items into two, three, or four equal parts. Drawing pictures of circles and squares is also very helpful:

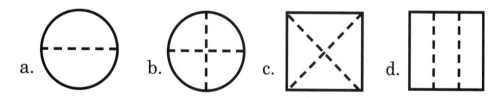

Ask your child if she knows what fractions the first circle (a) is divided into. Don't worry if she doesn't know—she probably won't. Explain that the first circle is divided into halves, which means two parts.

Then ask what fractions the second circle (b) is divided into. Explain that it is divided into quarters, which means four parts.

Now ask your child what fractions the first box (c) is divided into. It is also divided into quarters, because it has four parts.

Now ask her what fractions the next box (d) is divided into. It is divided into thirds, because it has three parts.

Ask your child to answer the following questions about the objects below.

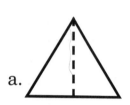 a.   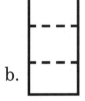 b.   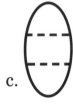 c.   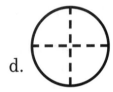 d.

1. Which one(s) of these shows thirds?

2. Which one of these shows quarters?

3. Which one of these shows halves?

If she got those right, give her one final set of questions about the objects below.

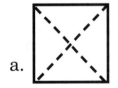 a.   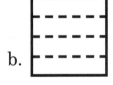 b.   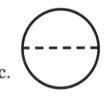 c.   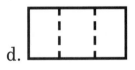 d.

1. Which one of these shows halves?

2. Which one(s) of these shows quarters?

3. Which one of these shows thirds?

If your child needs more help, you can make up problems using a pair of scissors, a few pieces of paper, and a few paper plates. Cut them into halves, thirds, and quarters, and then ask her to identify these fractions.

MINILESSON 37

Fractions: Part 2

In the previous minilesson, your child identified halves, thirds, and quarters. Now he will be dividing circles, squares, and other figures into halves, thirds, and quarters.

1. Have him divide this box into thirds:

2. Ask him to divide this group of balls into quarters (without dividing each ball):

3. Ask him to divide this pie in half:

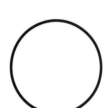

Answers:

1.

2.

3.

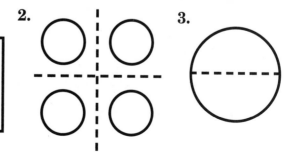

Money can also be used to illustrate fractions. Start with six pennies. Ask your child to divide the pennies in half. If he divides them into two sets of three, congratulate him. Then ask him to divide them into thirds.

Thirds may not be so easy. You may need to explain to him that this means dividing the pennies into three equal parts of two pennies each, like this:

Now put eight pennies in front of your child and ask him to divide them in half. If he divided them into two groups of four, tell him he is doing very well. Then ask him to divide them into quarters.

He should have divided them into four groups of two pennies each. If he did, have him try Problem Set A. If not, start again at the beginning of this minilesson.

Problem Set A

1. **a.** Divide the circle shown into halves.

    b. Then divide the circle into quarters.

2. Divide this box into thirds.

3. **a.** Divide this group of boxes in half.

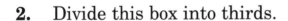

b. Divide this group of boxes into thirds.

c. Divide this group of boxes into quarters.

4. Put 16 pennies in front of your child and have him (a) divide them into halves; (b) divide them into quarters.

5. Put 20 pennies in front of your child and ask him to (a) divide them into halves; (b) divide them into quarters.

Answers on pages 109–110.

Answers to Chapter 14 Problem Set A

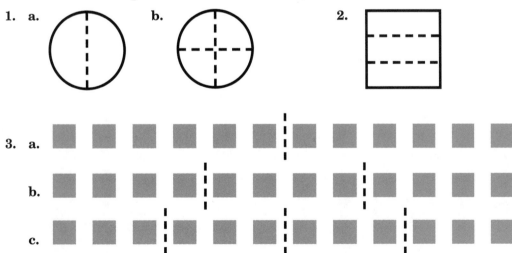

4. a.

b.

5. a.

b.

Chapter 15

Counting to 100

By the end of the first grade, your child should be able to count to 100 and to write all of those numbers. There are several ways to count to 100. In Minilesson 38, your child will count by 1s, from one to 100. In Minilesson 39, she will count by 2s, 5s, and 10s.

MINILESSON 38

Counting by 1s

There are two ways to find out if your child can do count to 100 by 1s and write all of those numbers. First, ask her to count up to 100. Usually, when young children get to 29, they'll let that nine go on for a couple of seconds—twenty-niiiiinnne, thirty, thirty-one, thirty-two. The reason for the slight delay is that they actually have to think about which number comes next. So it's perfectly normal if your child pauses for a few seconds at 29, 39, 49, 59, 69, 79, 89, and 99.

Then, after your child has successfully counted to 100, ask her to write down the numbers from 1 to 100 on a sheet of paper. If she can count to 100 and write the numbers from 1 to 100, then she's doing very well and you can go on to the next minilesson. But if she can't, you should give her some help.

The most effective way is to see where she gets stuck and then explain which number comes next. The key point is that counting up to 100 is almost the same as counting from 1 to 10, because the counting repeats itself after 20 (e.g., 21, 22, 23... 31, 32, 33...). Once you point this out, try counting together.

Since nearly every child loves to show off, it would be well worthwhile to ask your child to count up to 100—and even beyond 100—at least once a week. You can vary this exercise by having her count the number of cars that go by or the number of cans on a supermarket shelf. When we get to second-grade math, your child will be counting well past 100.

MINILESSON 39

Counting by 2s, 5s, and 10s

Everyone has heard this cheerful couplet:

Two, four, six, eight

Who do we appreciate?

What's really going on in this verse is counting by twos. While it's not essential that your child be able to count by 2s, 5s, and 10s by the end of the first grade, it adds to his facility with numbers. The more at ease he is with numbers, and the more he can manipulate them and make them work for him, the easier math will be in the later grades.

Counting by 2s, 5s, and 10s is the first step toward learning multiplication, which is the most important mathematical skill learned in the third grade. If your child can count by 2s, 5s, and 10s, then he can easily learn to multiply by 2, 5, and 10.

Let's start with 2s. Ask your child to count by 2s up to 100. If he gets stuck somewhere, write down that number, take a short break, and try again, beginning with 2, 4, 6, 8.

Whether or not your child gets it right on the first or even the second try, move on to writing by 2s all the numbers from 2 to 100 (i.e., 2, 4, 6, 8, ... 100).

Next have your child count by 5s up to 100. And then have him write all the numbers (i.e., 5, 10, 15, 20, ... 100).

Finally, have your child count by 10s up to 100. And then have him write all the numbers (i.e., 10, 20, 30, 40, ... 100).

de Final Exam

No automatic promotion here. There
im. First, this final should not be an
d to see if your child can do the work
no pocket calculators. Your child may
iem only to check her work. Let her
every problem twice. Children need to
efore they use machines.

This exam covers all the material in Minilessons 1 through
39—a whole year's work. So don't make your child do it all at one
sitting. It would be best if your child worked at this in six or
seven sessions of no more than half an hour each, perhaps
stretched out over about a week.

It's perfectly normal for your child to make some mistakes.
After all, nobody's perfect. If she makes just one mistake in any
section, you can definitely let it go. After all, 95 percent or 96 percent is a very good score. But if she makes three or four mistakes
in certain sections, then it would be best to repeat each minilesson involved and try the exam again later. The minilesson for
each section is given so that you can do this easily.

Answers on pages 128–132.

Chapter 1. Counting
(Minilessons 1 through 4, 38)

Write all the numbers from 1 to 100.

Chapter 2. Adding Single-Digit Numbers
(Minilessons 5 through 7)

Problem Set A

1. $2 + 2 = $ _____
2. $4 + 3 = $ _____
3. $1 + 6 = $ _____
4. $3 + 6 = $ _____

5. $4 + 5 = $ _____
6. $1 + 4 = $ _____
7. $6 + 2 = $ _____
8. $5 + 3 = $ _____

9. $1 + 8 = $ _____
10. $7 + 2 = $ _____
11. $3 + 2 = $ _____
12. $7 + 2 = $ _____

Problem Set B

1. $6 + 3 = $ _____
2. $8 + 1 = $ _____
3. $5 + 2 = $ _____
4. $1 + 6 = $ _____

5. $2 + 3 = $ _____
6. $5 + 3 = $ _____
7. $4 + 5 = $ _____
8. $2 + 7 = $ _____

9. $1 + 7 = $ _____
10. $1 + 5 = $ _____
11. $4 + 2 = $ _____
12. $2 + 3 = $ _____

Problem Set C

1. $5 + 6 = $ _____
2. $4 + 7 = $ _____
3. $3 + 9 = $ _____
4. $9 + 1 = $ _____

5. $3 + 7 = $ _____
6. $8 + 4 = $ _____
7. $5 + 9 = $ _____
8. $9 + 1 = $ _____

9. $8 + 3 = $ _____
10. $2 + 9 = $ _____
11. $4 + 9 = $ _____
12. $7 + 5 = $ _____

Chapter 3. Subtracting Single-Digit Numbers
(Minilessons 8 through 10)

Problem Set A

1. $6 - 1 =$ _____
2. $5 - 3 =$ _____
3. $3 - 1 =$ _____
4. $8 - 2 =$ _____

5. $6 - 3 =$ _____
6. $5 - 4 =$ _____
7. $9 - 6 =$ _____
8. $5 - 4 =$ _____

9. $7 - 4 =$ _____
10. $4 - 2 =$ _____
11. $2 - 1 =$ _____
12. $9 - 7 =$ _____

Problem Set B

1. $7 - 6 =$ _____
2. $9 - 2 =$ _____
3. $7 - 5 =$ _____
4. $8 - 3 =$ _____

5. $6 - 4 =$ _____
6. $9 - 1 =$ _____
7. $5 - 1 =$ _____
8. $6 - 5 =$ _____

9. $8 - 6 =$ _____
10. $5 - 3 =$ _____
11. $8 - 7 =$ _____
12. $9 - 4 =$ _____

Chapter 4. Building Math Skills
(Minilessons 12 and 13; no questions for Minilesson 11)

Introducing the Concept of 0 (Zero) (Minilesson 12)

1. $3 - 0 =$ _____
2. $1 + 0 =$ _____
3. $0 - 0 =$ _____

4. $5 - 5 =$ _____
5. $0 + 4 =$ _____
6. $7 - 0 =$ _____

7. $3 - 3 =$ _____
8. $1 - 0 =$ _____
9. $8 + 0 =$ _____

Filling in the Missing Number (Minilesson 13)

1. $4 + \underline{\hphantom{000}} = 6$ 6. $3 + \underline{\hphantom{000}} = 7$ 11. $8 - \underline{\hphantom{000}} = 8$

2. $3 + \underline{\hphantom{000}} = 8$ 7. $2 + \underline{\hphantom{000}} = 7$ 12. $9 - \underline{\hphantom{000}} = 2$

3. $1 + \underline{\hphantom{000}} = 9$ 8. $0 + \underline{\hphantom{000}} = 2$ 13. $2 - \underline{\hphantom{000}} = 0$

4. $3 + \underline{\hphantom{000}} = 3$ 9. $5 + \underline{\hphantom{000}} = 9$ 14. $4 - \underline{\hphantom{000}} = 3$

5. $8 + \underline{\hphantom{000}} = 9$ 10. $6 - \underline{\hphantom{000}} = 3$ 15. $7 - \underline{\hphantom{000}} = 5$

Chapter 5. Addition and Subtraction Drills
(Minilessons 14 and 15)

No questions.

Chapter 6. Addition into Double Digits
(Minilessons 16 and 17)

Adding Three Numbers (Minilesson 16)

1. $1 + 2 + 3 = \underline{\hphantom{000}}$ 5. $3 + 0 + 6 = \underline{\hphantom{000}}$ 9. $2 + 4 + 2 = \underline{\hphantom{000}}$

2. $4 + 3 + 2 = \underline{\hphantom{000}}$ 6. $5 + 2 + 1 = \underline{\hphantom{000}}$ 10. $3 + 3 + 3 = \underline{\hphantom{000}}$

3. $1 + 6 + 0 = \underline{\hphantom{000}}$ 7. $0 + 4 + 4 = \underline{\hphantom{000}}$ 11. $8 + 1 + 0 = \underline{\hphantom{000}}$

4. $2 + 2 + 2 = \underline{\hphantom{000}}$ 8. $1 + 7 + 1 = \underline{\hphantom{000}}$ 12. $6 + 1 + 2 = \underline{\hphantom{000}}$

Double-Digit Sums (Minilesson 17)

1. 15	**2.** 24	**3.** 16	**4.** 34
+63	+31	+21	+23

5. 22	**6.** 45	**7.** 57	**8.** 35
+15	+32	+41	+40

9. 32	**10.** 85	**11.** 20	**12.** 62
+53	+13	+76	+36

Chapter 7. Counting Money
(Minilessons 18 and 19)

1. How much is 5 cents plus two cents?

2. How much is 5 cents plus 4 cents?

3. How much is a nickel and a penny plus a nickel and two pennies?

4.   + =

5.   + =

6.

7. A dime plus four pennies = _____

8. A dime plus a nickel and two pennies = _____

9. ![coin] + ![coin] + ![coin] =

10. ![coin] + ![coin] + ![coin] =

11. ![coin] + ![coins] =

12. ![coin] + ![coin] + ![coins] =

Chapter 8. Word Problems with Single- and Double-Digit Numbers

(Minilessons 21 and 22, no questions for Minilesson 20)

1. How much is 4 plus 5?

2. How much is 8 minus 3?

3. If Joseph had three marbles and Melissa gave him four more, how many marbles does he have?

4. The Gold family ordered a pizza with eight slices. If they ate six slices, how many were left?

5. If Arlene kept two dolls on her bed, three on her dresser, and four in her toy chest, how many dolls did she have in all?

6. How much is 15 minus 4?

7. How much is 7 plus 12?

8. Julie had 9 cents. Bill gave her 8 cents. How much money does she now have?

9. Paula has 16 pairs of shoes. Five are black. How many are not black?

10. How much money is a dime, a nickel, and three pennies?

Chapter 9. Introduction to Telling Time
(Minilessons 23 and 24)

Problem Set A
What time is it on each of these clocks?

1. _____   2. _____   3. _____   4. _____

Problem Set B

Set your clock for each of these times:

1. six o'clock   **2.** twelve o'clock   **3.** half past five   **4.** half past one

Problem Set C

What time is it on each of these clocks?

1. _____   **2.** _____   **3.** _____

4. _____   **5.** _____   **6.** _____

Chapter 10. Double-Digit Addition and Subtraction

(Minilessons 25 through 27)

Double-Digit Addition (Minilessons 25 and 26)

1. 28	**2.** 72	**3.** 34	**4.** 20	**5.** 17
+31	+17	+22	+48	+31

6. 16	**7.** 29	**8.** 15	**9.** 46	**10.** 53
+13	+40	+71	+23	+41

Double-Digit Subtraction (Minilesson 27)

1. 42	**2.** 67	**3.** 58	**4.** 91
−20	−35	−22	−51

5. 75	**6.** 89	**7.** 48	**8.** 52
−62	−17	−11	−41

9. 38	**10.** 69	**11.** 99	**12.** 85
−26	−15	−27	−14

Chapter 11. Word Problems with and without Money

(Minilessons 28 and 29)

1. How much is 9 minus 8?

2. If George had four red balls, two yellow balls, and one brown ball, how many balls did he have in all?

3. Sarah had seven kittens. Five had stripes. How many did not have stripes?

4. How much is 5 plus 2 plus 2?

5. How much is 79 take away 34?

6. If Joan baked 39 cookies and gave away 25, how many cookies did she keep for herself?

7. How much is 57 cents minus 22 cents?

8. John left home in the morning with 97 cents. He returned home in the evening with 32 cents. How much money did John spend that day?

Chapter 12. Counting Pennies, Nickels, and Dimes

(Minilessons 30 and 31)

Problem Set A

1. How much is 94 cents minus 2 dimes and 2 pennies?

2. If you started with five dimes and nine pennies and ended up with 13 cents, how much money did you spend?

3. If George gave Stan and Irene a dime each and he had two dimes and a nickel left, how much money did he begin with?

4. Diane began the day with 78 cents. She gave a nickel to Marlene and a dime to Karen. How much money did she have left?

Problem Set B

1. How many dimes and pennies would you use to make 77 cents?

2. If you had 63 cents in dimes and pennies, how many dimes and how many pennies would you have?

3. If you had a dime, two nickels, and four pennies, how much money would you have?

4. If you had two quarters, a dime, and eight pennies, how much money would you have?

Problem Set C

1. How many dimes and pennies would you use to make 74 cents?

2. Six dimes make _____ cents.

3. If you had 82 cents in dimes and pennies, how many dimes and how many pennies would you have?

4. Two dimes make _____ cents.

5. How many dimes and pennies would you use to make 85 cents?

6. If you had a dime, a nickel, and two pennies, how much money would you have?

Problem Set D

For each of these, write down the amount of money shown:

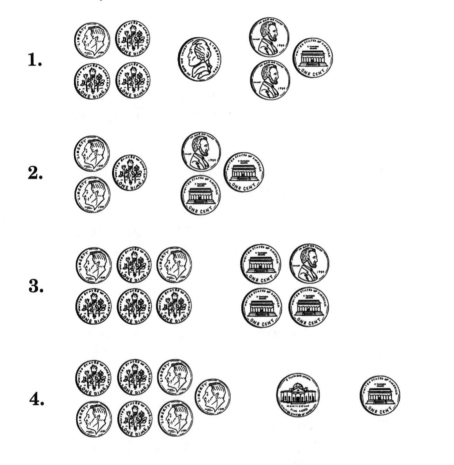

1.

2.

3.

4.

Chapter 13. Ordinal Numbers
(Minilessons 32 through 35)

Problem Set A

1. What is the sixth letter of the alphabet?

2. What is the eighth letter of the alphabet?

3. What is the fifth letter of the alphabet?

4. Which letter of the alphabet is G?

5. Which letter of the alphabet is B?

6. Which letter of the alphabet is J?

Problem Set B

1. Draw the third figure.

2. Draw the fifth figure.

3. Draw the sixth figure.

Problem Set C

Write the first 10 ordinal numbers as words.

_____   _____

_____   _____

_____   _____

_____   _____

_____   _____

Reading a Calendar (Minilesson 35)

October						
Sunday	Monday	Tuesday	Wednesday	Thursday	Friday	Saturday
					1	2
3	4	⑤	6	7	8	⑨
10	11	12	13	14	⑮	16
17	18	⑲	⑳	21	22	㉓
24	25	26	㉗	28	29	30
㉛						

1. Counting Sunday as the first day of the week, which day of the week is Thursday?

2. Counting Sunday as the first day of the week, which day of the week is Saturday?

3. Write (or name) each of the circled dates as an ordinal number.

Chapter 14. Introduction to Fractions
(Minilessons 36 and 37)

1.   Divide this square into quarters.

2.   Divide this circle into halves.

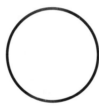

3.   Divide this group of boxes into thirds.

4.   Divide this rectangle into halves.

Chapter 15. Counting to 100
(Minilessons 38 and 39)

No questions.

First-Grade Final Exam Answers

Chapter 1. Counting

1, 2, 3, 4, 5, 6, 7, 8, 9, 10, 11, 12, 13, 14, 15, 16, 17, 18, 19, 20, 21, 22, 23, 24, 25, 26, 27, 28, 29, 30, 31, 32, 33, 34, 35, 36, 37, 38, 39, 40, 41, 42, 43, 44, 45, 46, 47, 48, 49, 50, 51, 52, 53, 54, 55, 56, 57, 58, 59, 60, 61, 62, 63, 64, 65, 66, 67, 68, 69, 70, 71, 72, 73, 74, 75, 76, 77, 78, 79, 80, 81, 82, 83, 84, 85, 86, 87, 88, 89, 90, 91, 92, 93, 94, 95, 96, 97, 98, 99, 100

Chapter 2. Adding Single-Digit Numbers

Problem Set A

1. 4	4. 9	7. 8	10. 9
2. 7	5. 9	8. 8	11. 5
3. 7	6. 5	9. 9	12. 9

Problem Set B

1. 9	4. 7	7. 9	10. 6
2. 9	5. 5	8. 9	11. 6
3. 7	6. 8	9. 8	12. 5

Problem Set C

1. 11	4. 10	7. 14	10. 11
2. 11	5. 10	8. 10	11. 13
3. 12	6. 12	9. 11	12. 12

Chapter 3. Subtracting Single-Digit Numbers

Problem Set A

1. 5	4. 6	7. 3	10. 2
2. 2	5. 3	8. 1	11. 1
3. 2	6. 1	9. 3	12. 2

Problem Set B

1. 1	4. 5	7. 4	10. 2
2. 7	5. 2	8. 1	11. 1
3. 2	6. 8	9. 2	12. 5

Chapter 4. Building Math Skills

Introducing the Concept of 0 (Zero)

1. 3   **4.** 0   **7.** 0
2. 1   **5.** 4   **8.** 1
3. 0   **6.** 7   **9.** 8

Filling in the Missing Number

1. 2   **5.** 1   **9.** 4   **13.** 2   **17.** 0
2. 5   **6.** 4   **10.** 3   **14.** 1   **18.** 5
3. 8   **7.** 5   **11.** 0   **15.** 2
4. 0   **8.** 2   **12.** 7   **16.** 8

Chapter 5. Addition and Subtraction Drills

No questions.

Chapter 6. Addition into Double Digits

Adding Three Numbers

1. 6   **4.** 6   **7.** 8   **10.** 9
2. 9   **5.** 9   **8.** 9   **11.** 9
3. 7   **6.** 8   **9.** 8   **12.** 9

Double-Digit Sums

1. 78   **4.** 57   **7.** 98   **10.** 98
2. 55   **5.** 37   **8.** 75   **11.** 96
3. 37   **6.** 77   **9.** 85   **12.** 98

Chapter 7. Counting Money

1. 7 cents   **5.** 14 cents   **9.** 16 cents
2. 9 cents   **6.** 19 cents   **10.** 13 cents
3. 13 cents   **7.** 14 cents   **11.** 17 cents
4. 12 cents   **8.** 17 cents   **12.** 19 cents

Chapter 8. Word Problems with Single- and Double-Digit Numbers

1. 9
2. 5
3. seven marbles (3 + 4 = 7)
4. two slices (8 − 6 = 2)
5. nine dolls (2 + 3 + 4 = 9)

6. 11
7. 19
8. 17 cents (9 + 8 = 17)
9. 11 pairs (16 − 5 = 11)
10. 18 cents (10 + 5 + 3 = 18)

Chapter 9. Introduction to Telling Time

Problem Set A
1. five o'clock, or 5:00
2. eleven o'clock, or 11:00
3. half past eight, 8:30 or eight thirty
4. half past four, 4:30 or four thirty

Problem Set B

1.   **2.**   **3.**   **4.**

Problem Set C
1. half past ten, or ten thirty
2. six o'clock
3. half past four, or four thirty
4. half past one, or one thirty
5. eleven o'clock
6. seven o'clock

Chapter 10. Double-Digit Addition and Subtraction

Double-Digit Addition
1. 59   **3.** 56   **5.** 48   **7.** 69   **9.** 69
2. 89   **4.** 68   **6.** 29   **8.** 86   **10.** 94

Double-Digit Subtraction
1. 22   **4.** 40   **7.** 37   **10.** 54
2. 32   **5.** 13   **8.** 11   **11.** 72
3. 36   **6.** 72   **9.** 12   **12.** 71

Chapter 11. Word Problems with and without Money

1. 9
   -8
   1

2. 4
   $+2$
   $+1$
   7 balls

3. 7
   -5
   2 kittens

4. 5
   $+2$
   $+2$
   9

5. 79
   -34
   45

6. 39
   -25
   14 cookies

7. 57
   -22
   35 cents

8. 97
   -32
   65 cents

Chapter 12. Counting Pennies, Nickels, and Dimes

Problem Set A

1. 94
   -22
   72 cents

2. 59
   -13
   46 cents
   (four dimes
   and six
   pennies)

3. 10
   $+10$
   $+10$
   $+10$
   $+ 5$
   45 cents

4. 5   78
   $+10$ -15
   15   63 cents

Problem Set B

1. seven dimes
   and seven
   pennies

2. six dimes
   and three
   pennies

3. 10
   $+ 5$
   $+ 5$
   $+ 4$
   24 cents

4. 25
   $+25$
   $+10$
   $+ 8$
   68 cents

Problem Set C

1. seven dimes and four pennies
2. 60
3. eight dimes and two pennies
4. 20
5. eight dimes and five pennies

Problem Set D

1. 48 cents **2.** 33 cents **3.** 64 cents **4.** 76 cents

Chapter 15. Ordinal Numbers

Problem Set A

1. F
2. H
3. E
4. seventh
5. second
6. 10th

Problem Set B

1. 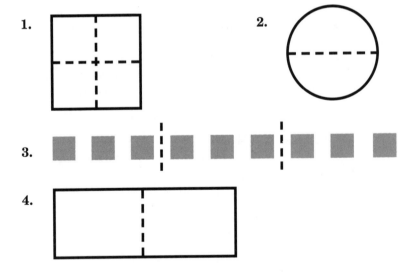   2.   3.

Problem Set C

first   sixth
second   seventh
third   eighth
fourth   ninth
fifth   tenth

Reading a Calendar

1. fifth
2. seventh
3. fifth, or 5th; ninth, or 9th; fifteenth, or 15th; nineteenth, or 19th; twentieth, or 20th; twenty-third, or 23rd; twenty-seventh, or 27th; thirty-first, or 31st

Chapter 14. Fractions

1.   2.

3.

4.

Chapter 15. Counting to 100

No questions.

Last Word in First Grade

The fundamentals of first-grade math are addition and subtraction. If your child has mastered these two fundamental skills, then she or he may go directly to second-grade mathematics.

Remember that simple addition and subtraction are two of the basic building blocks of mathematics and must be put firmly in place so that we can build on them. Hey, if Einstein had trouble with basic math when he was a kid, then there's nothing wrong with your kid taking a little extra time to learn the fundamentals. After all, as Einstein himself pointed out, all things are relative.

PART II
Second-Grade Math

Introduction to Second-Grade Math

"What did you do on your summer vacation?" Every fall when children return to schools all across the nation, many of them are asked to write this composition. Indeed, this may be the most widely assigned composition title of all time. The children write about travel, attending day camp or sleep-away camp, playing with their friends, visiting relatives, and a whole variety of other activities. But you can be sure that very few children mention studying math.

Consequently, most elementary school teachers spend about three weeks each September reviewing the math covered in the previous grade. Indeed, this review is generally built into the curriculum. At this juncture, now that you and your child have worked your way through first-grade math, you certainly won't need to spend three weeks reviewing this material if you're not taking two months off the way our schools do each summer.

We know from sad experience that the study of mathematics is not analogous to the adage about learning to ride a bicycle: Once you learn to ride, you never forget. Learning mathematics is more analogous to the old adage, If you don't use it, you lose it. So while it's fine to take off a few days here and there, or even a week or two at a time, if your child is going to master all the material covered in this book, it's necessary to work at it on a regular basis.

Much of what is taught in the second grade is an extension of first-grade math—counting, addition, and subtraction. Multiplication and division are introduced, but very briefly. Second-graders are also given a very brief introduction to statistics, probability, and geometry.

By the end of the second grade, your child should be able to count from 1 to 1,000. Once we get past 100, the rest is very easy. Your child should also be able to count by 2s, 3s, 4s, 5s, and 10s, as this enhances her ability to manipulate numbers and eventually to learn the multiplication table, which is introduced in the third grade.

As your child's ability to read continues to grow, she will be able to work more and more independently. After Chapter 20, I shall assume that your child is doing most of the reading and that you're more or less in the background, ready to step in to help.

What you might do, then, is read each minilesson, then ask your child to do it. When she is finished, ask her if she got stuck. Help her with any areas she is unsure of. You should also check her work when she has finished each minilesson. Since solutions are provided for every problem, in most cases she will be able to check her own work. However, you want to make sure that she is doing every minilesson and that she does understand all the work.

It may still be necessary from time to time to repeat a minilesson. Your child may be reluctant to do this. So that's still another reason you need to monitor your child's progress. Keep in mind that this book covers two full years of math, so you're moving very quickly if you cover more than two or three minilessons in a week.

How many minilessons should be covered in a week and how long should be spent on each minilesson? If your child has a very good week or does not have to repeat any minilessons, as many as five or six could be covered. I would recommend spending an average of 20 minutes to half an hour on most minilessons, but keep in mind that some children work faster than others.

I want to remind you that there's no need to race through this book. Your child may have to repeat some minilessons and some entire chapters. If your child needs to go over a certain concept three or four times before she has it down, that's time well spent. And you can reinforce the learning of these concepts by making up your own problems. And then make a game of it by having your child make up some additional problems.

As in first grade, your child should not use a pocket calculator. Seven- and eight-year-olds are using them today, and your child may wonder why she can't use one since it's certainly a lot faster and easier to do math problems with a pocket calculator. The reason is that when young children depend on calculators, they never really learn to do addition and subtraction. Children learn math by actually doing it, either in their heads or with pencil and paper. And as they get better and better at solving problems, they won't even be tempted to use a calculator.

Now it's time to get your child started on second-grade math. She'll need your help for the first five chapters or so, but then she should be able to work more independently.

Chapter 16

Counting and Writing Numbers up to 200

By the end of the second grade, your child should be able to count from 1 to 1,000. He can start by counting up to 200 and writing these numbers, and then spelling the numbers from 1 to 50.

In Minilesson 40, your child will recite all the numbers from 1 to 200 and then write each of these numbers. Minilesson 41 will cover writing the words for the numbers from 1 to 50.

Counting and Writing Numbers from 1 to 200

Ask your child to count from 1 to 200. If he has any trouble, read the following Extra Help box. If he can do it, skip the box.

EXTRA HELP

Counting to 200

How high can your child count without making a mistake? If your child can count to 100, then all you need to explain is that going beyond that number means just placing the words *one hundred* in front of 1, 2, and 3. So your child needs to practice saying, "One hundred and one, one hundred and two, one hundred and three," and so on.

If your child cannot yet count to 100, you'll need to review with him Minilessons 1 through 4, 38, and 39. After you've done this, and your child can count to 100, then explain to him that counting from 101 to 200 just entails placing the words *one hundred* in front of each number.

Now give him a couple of pieces of paper and a pencil and have him write all the numbers from 1 to 200.

If your child got everything right, go on to Minilesson 41. If not, your child can check his work with Table 4. After he does this, go over his mistakes with him. When you feel he's ready, have him begin a few numbers before where he made his first mistake and redo the rest of the numbers.

TABLE 4
The Numbers 1 to 200

1	26	51	76	101	126	151	176
2	27	52	77	102	127	152	177
3	28	53	78	103	128	153	178
4	29	54	79	104	129	154	179
5	30	55	80	105	130	155	180
6	31	56	81	106	131	156	181
7	32	57	82	107	132	157	182
8	33	58	83	108	133	158	183
9	34	59	84	109	134	159	184
10	35	60	85	110	135	160	185
11	36	61	86	111	136	161	186
12	37	62	87	112	137	162	187
13	38	63	88	113	138	163	188
14	39	64	89	114	139	164	189
15	40	65	90	115	140	165	190
16	41	66	91	116	141	166	191
17	42	67	92	117	142	167	192
18	43	68	93	118	143	168	193
19	44	69	94	119	144	169	194
20	45	70	95	120	145	170	195
21	46	71	96	121	146	171	196
22	47	72	97	122	147	172	197
23	48	73	98	123	148	173	198
24	49	74	99	124	149	174	199
25	50	75	100	125	150	175	200

Writing the Words for the Numbers from 1 to 50

Now your child will be writing the words that go with each of the numbers from 1 to 50. We'll start with the words that go with the numbers from 1 to 20. I'll get her started:

1 one _____   11 _____

2 _____   12 _____

3 _____   13 _____

4 _____   14 _____

5 _____   15 _____

6 _____   16 _____

7 _____   17 _____

8 _____   18 _____

9 _____   19 _____

10 _____   20 _____

Answers:

1 one   11 eleven

2 two   12 twelve

3 three   13 thirteen

4 four   14 fourteen

5 five   15 fifteen

6 six   16 sixteen

7 seven   17 seventeen

8 eight   18 eighteen

9 nine   19 nineteen

10 ten   20 twenty

Does spelling count? Not in this book. While I think it would be a good idea to correct your child's spelling, we have enough to worry about just getting the numbers right.

Now have her write the numbers from 21 to 50, and next to each number, write the word. I'll start off:

21 twenty-one   31 thirty-one   _____

22 twenty-two   _____   _____

_____   _____   _____

_____   _____   _____

_____   _____   _____

_____   _____   _____

_____   _____   _____

_____   _____   _____

_____   _____

Answers:

21 twenty-one	31 thirty-one	41 forty-one
22 twenty-two	32 thirty-two	42 forty-two
23 twenty-three	33 thirty-three	43 forty-three
24 twenty-four	34 thirty-four	44 forty-four
25 twenty-five	35 thirty-five	45 forty-five
26 twenty-six	36 thirty-six	46 forty-six
27 twenty-seven	37 thirty-seven	47 forty-seven
28 twenty-eight	38 thirty-eight	48 forty-eight
29 twenty-nine	39 thirty-nine	49 forty-nine
30 thirty	40 forty	50 fifty

Chapter 17

Mathematical Symbols

In mathematics, symbols are a shorthand way of expressing relationships between numbers. For instance, the sign = means that the number or numbers on one side of an equation is or are equal to the number or numbers on the other side. In Minilessons 42 through 44, we'll introduce and use several symbols that will help your child understand mathematical relationships.

MINILESSON 42

Greater Than and Less Than

Make sure your child knows these mathematical symbols:

> \+ means plus
> – means minus
> = means equals

If he has these down, he's ready to learn two more signs:

> \> means greater than
> < means less than

For instance, 8 > 6 reads: Eight is greater than six. And 3 < 9 reads: Three is less than nine.

Make sure your child can read and understand all of these signs, because they'll keep coming up in mathematics texts. Tell him to think of the symbol for greater than or less than as the greedy mouth that always wants to eat the greater, or bigger, number. This kind of trick may help him remember what this symbol means. So if he sees 4 < 10, the greedy mouth is eating the greater number, the 10. So 4 is less than 10. If he sees 3 > 1, the mouth has turned to eat the 3 because it's greater than the 1.

Have your child fill in these two blank spaces:

9 > 5 means that 9 _____ 5.

2 < 8 means that 2 _____ 8.

Did he answer them this way: 9 is greater than 5; 2 is less than 8?

If not, review the terms again. If so, have your child fill in all the blanks in Problem Set A.

Problem Set A

1. 3 + 3 means 3 _____ 3.

2. 8 > 4 means 8 _____ 4.

3. 5 − 4 means 5 _____ 4.

4. 5 < 6 means 5 _____ 6.

5. 8 − 3 means 8 _____ 3.

6. 4 < 6 means 4 _____ 6.

7. 7 > 1 means 7 _____ 1.

8. 2 + 3 means 2 _____ 3.

9. 4 = 4 means 4 _____ 4.

10. 9 > 7 means 9 _____ 7.

11. 8 = 8 means 8 _____ 8.

Answers on page 150.

If your child got all these right, go directly to Minilesson 43. If not, you'll need to redo this minilesson with him. Recognizing mathematical symbols is crucial to mastering arithmetic.

MINILESSON 43

Equal To and Not Equal To

Now you'll teach your child to apply the mathematical symbols you reviewed in the last minilesson to some larger numbers. And it's time to add a new symbol, $\neq$, which means not equal.

To illustrate the concept of "not equal" to your child, go through these three problems together. Is each of these sets of numbers equal (=) or not equal ($\neq$)? Write the correct symbol in the box in each problem.

1. $10 \ \square \ 6 + 5$

2. $5 + 9 \ \square \ 7 + 7$

3. $10 + 7 \ \square \ 5 + 11$

Answers:
1. $\neq$ **2.** =   **3.** $\neq$

Let's look at each of these problems:

1. Is 10 equal to the sum of $6 + 5$? How much is the sum of $6 + 5$? It's 11. So $10 \neq 11$.

2. Is the sum of $5 + 9$ equal to the sum of $7 + 7$? The sum of $5 + 9$ is 14. The sum of $7 + 7$ is 14. So the two sides are equal: $14 = 14$.

3. Is the sum of $10 + 7$ equal to the sum of $5 + 11$? The sum of $10 + 7$ is 17. The sum of $5 + 11$ is 16. So $17 \neq 16$.

Problem Set B

Have your child use > or < to complete each statement.

1. 7 ☐ 5   **5.** 8 ☐ 4

2. 4 ☐ 6   **6.** 7 ☐ 6

3. 9 ☐ 2   **7.** 4 ☐ 5

4. 5 ☐ 8   **8.** 1 ☐ 2

Answers on page 150.

Problem Set C

Now have your child try something a little bit different. Have her answer using these symbols: =, <, and >.

1. 12 + 6 ☐ 8 + 9   **5.** 9 + 8 ☐ 5 + 12

2. 15 + 4 ☐ 9 + 10   **6.** 3 + 14 ☐ 8 + 11

3. 11 + 8 ☐ 6 + 12   **7.** 5 + 14 ☐ 11 + 7

4. 4 + 9 ☐ 6 + 8   **8.** 4 + 13 ☐ 6 + 10

Answers on page 150.

Problem Set D

Here your child has to combine a couple of operations. Answer with >, <, or =.

1. 3 ☐ 9 − 7   **5.** 8 ☐ 1 + 6

2. 4 ☐ 2 + 3   **6.** 5 ☐ 8 − 3

3. 6 ☐ 9 − 3   **7.** 2 ☐ 8 − 6

4. 3 ☐ 7 − 5   **8.** 2 ☐ 8 − 5

Answers on page 150.

Check your child's answers. If she got them all right, then go on to Problem Set E. But if she got even one wrong, have her try the last set over again. If she still gets the same one wrong, then go over it with her until she understands all the symbols and how to solve for them. If she is getting frustrated, it's time to let it rest for a day or so until she is ready to try again.

Problem Set E

Use the symbols = and ≠ to answer these problems:

1. $14 - 7$ ☐ $18 - 11$ 4. $13 - 4$ ☐ $18 - 9$

2. $16 - 9$ ☐ $19 - 12$ 5. $12 - 7$ ☐ $9 - 4$

3. $12 - 4$ ☐ $19 - 10$ 6. $15 - 6$ ☐ $10 - 3$

Answers on page 150.

Problem Set F

Have your child use these symbols: =, >, and <.

1. $15 - 7$ ☐ $19 - 10$ 4. $12 - 8$ ☐ $6 - 2$

2. $14 - 5$ ☐ $17 - 8$ 5. $9 - 3$ ☐ $17 - 12$

3. $16 - 11$ ☐ $12 - 7$ 6. $18 - 7$ ☐ $12 - 2$

Answers on page 150.

MINILESSON 44

Addition and Subtraction Problems with Symbols

Now let's see how well your child understands the symbols that were introduced in the last two minilessons. We'll be combining addition and subtraction.

Problem Set G

Have your child use the symbols = and ≠ to work out these relationships:

1. 9 + 4 ☐ 7 + 7   **5.** 12 − 7 ☐ 18 − 13

2. 13 − 4 ☐ 6 + 3   **6.** 19 − 6 ☐ 5 + 9

3. 15 − 5 ☐ 4 + 6   **7.** 2 + 13 ☐ 17 − 2

4. 3 + 14 ☐ 19 − 3   **8.** 9 + 6 ☐ 19 − 5

Answers on page 150.

Problem Set H

Now have your child use the symbols >, <, and = to answer these problems:

1. 15 − 7 ☐ 3 + 5   **8.** 15 − 3 ☐ 6 + 7

2. 11 + 3 ☐ 19 − 7   **9.** 5 + 6 ☐ 17 − 5

3. 4 + 9 ☐ 18 − 4   **10.** 18 − 7 ☐ 5 + 7

4. 4 + 7 ☐ 16 − 6   **11.** 12 + 5 ☐ 19 − 3

5. 16 − 8 ☐ 4 + 6   **12.** 9 + 4 ☐ 18 − 5

6. 7 + 6 ☐ 18 − 5   **13.** 2 + 14 ☐ 19 − 4

7. 19 − 4 ☐ 6 + 8   **14.** 16 − 7 ☐ 2 + 8

Answers on page 150.

Answers to Chapter 17 Problem Sets

Problem Set A

1. 3 plus 3
2. 8 is greater than 4
3. 5 minus (or take away) 4
4. 5 is less than 6
5. 8 minus (or take away) 3
6. 4 is less than 6
7. 7 is greater than 1
8. 2 plus 3
9. 4 equals (or is equal to) 4
10. 9 is greater than 7
11. 8 equals (or is equal to) 8

Problem Set B

1. $7 > 5$
2. $4 < 6$
3. $9 > 2$
4. $5 < 8$
5. $8 > 4$
6. $7 > 6$
7. $4 < 5$
8. $1 < 2$

Problem Set C

1. $18 > 17$
2. $19 = 19$
3. $19 > 18$
4. $13 < 14$
5. $17 = 17$
6. $17 < 19$
7. $19 > 18$
8. $17 > 16$

Problem Set D

1. $3 > 9 - 7 (= 2)$
2. $4 < 2 + 3 (= 5)$
3. $6 = 9 - 3 (= 6)$
4. $3 > 7 - 5 (= 2)$
5. $8 > 1 + 6 (= 7)$
6. $5 = 8 - 3 (= 5)$
7. $2 = 8 - 6 (= 2)$
8. $2 < 8 - 5 (= 3)$

Problem Set E

1. $7 = 7$
2. $7 = 7$
3. $8 \neq 9$
4. $9 = 9$
5. $5 = 5$
6. $9 \neq 7$

Problem Set F

1. $8 < 9$
2. $9 = 9$
3. $5 = 5$
4. $4 = 4$
5. $6 > 5$
6. $11 > 10$

Problem Set G

1. $13 \neq 14$
2. $9 = 9$
3. $10 = 10$
4. $17 \neq 16$
5. $5 = 5$
6. $13 \neq 14$
7. $15 = 15$
8. $15 \neq 14$

Problem Set H

1. $8 = 8$
2. $14 > 12$
3. $13 < 14$
4. $11 > 10$
5. $8 < 10$
6. $13 = 13$
7. $15 > 14$
8. $12 < 13$
9. $11 < 12$
10. $11 < 12$
11. $17 > 16$
12. $13 = 13$
13. $16 > 15$
14. $9 < 10$

Grouping Numbers in 10s and 1s

Ask your child if she knows how many dimes there are in 40 cents. If she answers that there are four dimes, ask how many pennies there are in 6 cents. She should know that there are six.

Now ask how many dimes and how many pennies there are in 46 cents. If she learned her money lessons well, she should know that there are four dimes and six pennies.

We'll be working out problems like these in Minilesson 45, when we break down numbers into 10s and 1s. Some children have an easier time learning how to break down a number into 10s and 1s by actually seeing boxes on a graph. In Minilesson 46, we'll show how a number can be broken down into tens and ones on a graph. And then, in Minilesson 47, we'll add numbers by adding boxes on a graph.

MINILESSON 45

10s and 1s: Part 1

This minilesson will be expensive. You'll need nine dimes and nine pennies before you even get started.

Your child already knows that there are 10 cents to a dime. Now you can reinforce that knowledge by working with 10s and 1s.

First, ask your child how many dimes and how many pennies there are in 75 cents. If necessary, break this up into two problems: How many dimes are there in 70 cents, and then, how many pennies are there in 5 cents? Ask him to place 75 cents in dimes and pennies in front of him. He should have placed seven dimes and five pennies in front of him. Ask him how many cents to a dime. And how many cents to a penny. Since there are 10 cents to a dime, we can think of a dime as 10. And since there is one cent to a penny, we can think of a penny as 1.

Ask your child how many 10s and 1s make 75 cents. Try to have him answer in 10s and 1s instead of dimes and pennies. There are seven 10s and five 1s in 75 cents.

Now ask how many 10s and 1s make 53 cents. If he knows there are five 10s and three 1s, go on to the next paragraph. If he doesn't, have him place the five dimes and three pennies in front of him, and then ask how many 10s and 1s make 53.

Ask your child how many 10s and 1s there are in 67 cents. If he knows there are six 10s and seven 1s in 67, go directly to the next paragraph. If he doesn't, then have him place the right number of dimes and pennies in from of him to make the number 67. If he places six dimes and seven pennies in front of him, then ask how many 10s and how many 1s make up 67.

Now have your child write the whole numbers that are made up of these 10s and 1s:

1. three 10s, four 1s = _____

2. six 10s, two 1s = _____

3. four 10s, three 1s = _____

Answers:
1. 34   **2.** 62   **3.** 43

Now have your child do Problem Sets A and B.

Problem Set A

Fill in each of these:

1. 29 = _____ 10s, _____ 1s

2. 74 = _____ 10s, _____ 1s

3. 58 = _____ 10s, _____ 1s

4. 44 = _____ 10s, _____ 1s

5. 16 = _____ 10s, _____ 1s

6. 39 = _____ 10s, _____ 1s

7. 77 = _____ 10s, _____ 1s

For each of these, write in the number:

8. seven 10s, one 1 = _____

9. eight 10s, zero 1s = _____

10. four 10s, seven 1s = _____

11. nine 10s, three 1s = _____

12. six 10s, four 1s = _____

13. one 10, nine 1s = _____

14. zero 10s, eight 1s = _____

Answers on page 159.

Problem Set B

1. In the number 65 there are _____ 10s and _____ 1s.

2. In the number 48 there are _____ 10s and _____ 1s.

3. In the number 86 there are _____ 10s and _____ 1s.

4. In the number 96 there are _____ 10s and _____ 1s.

5. In the number 73 there are _____ 10s and _____ 1s.

6. What number has eight 10s and two 1s?

7. What number has two 10s and six 1s?

8. What number has six 10s and one 1?

9. What number has four 10s and four 1s?

10. What number has nine 10s and four 1s?

Answers on page 159.

If your child needs more work, read the following Extra Help box with him. Grouping numbers into 10s and 1s is a very important mathematical skill that needs to be mastered before the end of the second grade.

Working with 10s and 1s

Ask your child, "How many cents does a dime have?" He should know that it has 10 cents.

Now ask, "How many dimes are there in 30 cents?"
Answer: There are three dimes in 30 cents.

Now ask your child, "How many cents is a penny equal to?"
Answer: A penny is equal to 1 cent.

Now ask how many dimes and how many pennies there are in 48 cents.
Answer: There are four dimes and eight pennies.

Have your child place four dimes and eight pennies in front of him. Now ask him: "If a dime is 10 and a penny is 1, how many 10s and how many 1s are there are in 48?" If he knows there are four 10s and eight 1s in 48, you can go directly to Minilesson 46.

If he's unsure, here's another problem for your child to do: How many 10s and how many 1s are there in 84? If he knows the answer is eight 10s and four 1s, then he's ready for the next minilesson. If he doesn't know, ask him to use dimes and pennies to help him find the answer. If he places eight dimes and four pennies in front of him, he should quickly realize that there are eight 10s and four 1s in 84. If he still doesn't understand, then it's probably a good idea to take a break and repeat this Extra Help box and Minilesson 45 later.

MINILESSON 46

10s and 1s: Part 2

Your child knows that there are ten 1s in one 10. But seeing is usually believing. So in this minilesson, we'll represent 1s and 10s with boxes. You'll need six pieces of plain white paper.

Have your child figure out how many boxes are shown here →

There are 14 boxes. Ask her how she got her answer. Did she count all the boxes? There's a much faster way: Put these boxes into two groups: 10s and 1s. Since there is one group of 10s and four 1s, there is a total of 14 boxes.

Explain to her that it's much faster to go 10 + 4 = 14 than to count 1, 2, 3, 4, 5, 6, 7, 8, 9, 10, 11, 12, 13, 14.

Now have her figure out how many boxes are here →

There are 25 boxes. Ask your child, "What does this part of the number 25 mean?" (Point to the 2 in 25.) Ask her to shade in the boxes that correspond to the 2 in 25. If she shades in 20 boxes, then go to the next problem. If she doesn't, then explain that the 2 in 25 stands for the two columns of 10 boxes—the two 10s.

Now ask her how many boxes there are in this problem →

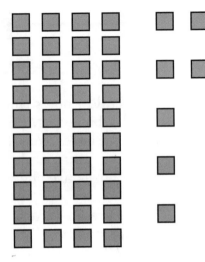

There are 47 boxes.

Now let's reverse the process. Have your child draw the following groups of boxes on a piece of paper. You'll have to check these yourself.

1. Draw 58 boxes in groups of 10s and 1s.

2. Draw 61 boxes in groups of 10s and 1s.

3. Draw 39 boxes in groups of 10s and 1s.

4. Draw 55 boxes in groups of 10s and 1s.

5. Draw 79 boxes in groups of 10s and 1s.

6. Draw 50 boxes in a group of 10s.

MINILESSON 47

Adding by Grouping

In the last two minilessons, we learned how to break whole numbers down into 10s and 1s, and to show these 10s and 1s graphically. Now we're going to do some addition using groups of 10s and 1s.

Ask your child to add these numbers:

$$23$$
$$+45$$

She should be able to get 68. Show her another way to think about this problem, using boxes to group the numbers into 10s and 1s.

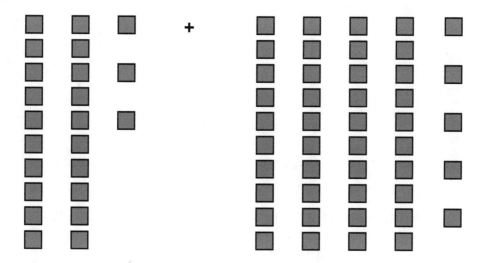

Twenty-three is really two groups of 10s and a group of three 1s. And 45 consists of four groups of 10s and a group of five 1s. If we put them together, we have six groups of 10s and a group of eight 1s.

Now ask your child to add these numbers:

$$34$$
$$+52$$

Answer: 86

Here's how this same problem can be solved with groups of 10s and 1s:

Three groups of 10s   +   five groups of 10s
and a group of four 1s: and a group of two 1s:

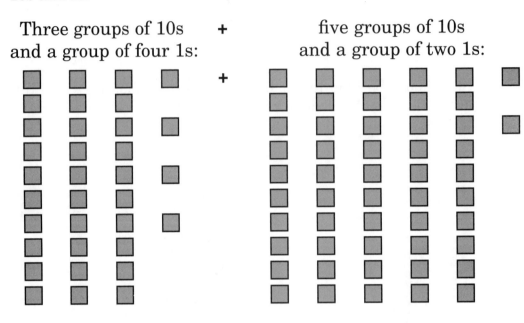

equals eight groups of 10s and a group of six 1s:

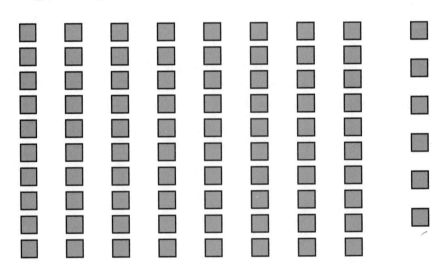

equals 86.

A second explanation is to show how you can add:

$$
\begin{array}{r}
34 \\
+52 \\
\hline
86
\end{array}
$$

Four plus two equals six 1s, and three 10s plus five 10s equals eight 10s.

Answers to Chapter 18 Problem Sets

Problem Set A

1.	two 10s, nine 1s	8.	71
2.	seven 10s, four 1s	9.	80
3.	five 10s, eight 1s	10.	47
4.	four 10s, four 1s	11.	93
5.	one 10, six 1s	12.	64
6.	three 10s, nine 1s	13.	19
7.	seven 10s, seven 1s	14.	8

Problem Set B

1.	six 10s, five 1s	6.	82
2.	four 10s, eight 1s	7.	26
3.	eight 10s, six 1s	8.	61
4.	nine 10s, six 1s	9.	44
5.	seven 10s, three 1s	10.	94

Chapter 19

Adding Three Numbers and Double- and Triple-Digit Numbers

In Minilessons 48 through 50 we'll be reviewing some first-grade addition and then carrying that addition a few steps further.

MINILESSON 48

Adding Three Numbers

Ask your child to add:

$$4 + 2 + 5 = \underline{\hspace{2cm}}$$

What did she get? $4 + 2 + 5 = 11$. Remind her that she can break it up into two problems: $4 + 2 = 6$; $6 + 5 = 11$.

Now try this one:

$$6 + 3 + 7 = \underline{\hspace{2cm}}$$

What did she get? $6 + 3 + 7 = 16$. Or, $6 + 3 = 9$; $9 + 7 = 16$.

Now have your child try Problem Set A.

Problem Set A				
1. 3 +4 +3	**2.** 6 +2 +4	**3.** 5 +5 +3	**4.** 7 +4 +6	**5.** 2 +8 +0

6. 9	**7.** 7	**8.** 3	**9.** 0	**10.** 8
+8	+4	+3	+4	+8
+1	+5	+8	+9	+2

11. 1	**12.** 6	**13.** 6	**14.** 9	**15.** 7
+4	+8	+6	+5	+7
+9	+3	+6	+4	+5

Answers on page 164.

MINILESSON 49

Adding Double-Digit Numbers

Can your child add these two numbers?

24
+32

Did she get 56? If she did, she's ready to do Problem Set B. If she did not get 56, help her work out that problem. And then find the answer to this one:

34
+25

Answer: 34
             +25
             59

All we did here was add 4 and 5 to get 9, and then we added three 10s and two 10s to get five 10s. Put them together and we have 59. It's as easy as that!

Now have your child do Problem Set B.

Problem Set B

1. 21
+48

2. 37
+22

3. 11
+17

4. 14
+13

5. 46
+21

6. 53
+42

7. 31
+38

8. 50
+29

9. 73
+12

10. 10
+64

11. 35
+24

12. 64
+23

13. 49
+20

14. 20
+30

15. 16
+52

16. 29
+40

17. 32
+61

18. 55
+33

Answers on page 164.

MINILESSON 50

Adding Triple-Digit Numbers

Adding triple-digit numbers is a little more work than adding double-digit numbers, but your child should not find this any harder. In Chapter 23 we'll be doing addition with carrying, so it is very important for him to be able to handle the problems in this minilesson with ease.

We're going to be moving into larger numbers: 100s. Ask your child, "How many 1s are in 100?" There are one hundred 1s in 100.

Now ask, "How many 10s are in 100?" There are ten 10s in 100.

Now ask your child to count by 100s from 100 to 900.

Answer: 100, 200, 300, 400, 500, 600, 700, 800, 900.

Your child will be getting familiar with 100s by using them in addition problems in this minilesson and in subtraction problems in the next minilesson. Now have your child try to add these numbers:

$$146$$
$$+123$$

Did he get 269? Here's one more:

$$234$$
$$+453$$

Did your child get 687? If he got these two problems right, then he's definitely ready for Problem Set C. If he didn't, then you'll need to review Minilessons 25 and 26 with him.

Problem Set C

1. 116 +213	**2.** 234 +245	**3.** 137 +441	**4.** 382 +417	**5.** 155 +641
6. 320 +465	**7.** 415 +184	**8.** 138 +210	**9.** 807 +141	**10.** 572 +314
11. 153 +533	**12.** 610 +377	**13.** 561 +226	**14.** 330 +459	**15.** 425 +463

Answers on page 164.

Answers to Chapter 19 Problem Sets

Problem Set A

1. 10	**2.** 12	**3.** 13	**4.** 17	**5.** 10
6. 18	**7.** 16	**8.** 14	**9.** 13	**10.** 18
11. 14	**12.** 17	**13.** 18	**14.** 18	**15.** 19

Problem Set B

1. 69	**2.** 59	**3.** 28	**4.** 27	**5.** 67
6. 95	**7.** 69	**8.** 79	**9.** 85	**10.** 74
11. 59	**12.** 87	**13.** 69	**14.** 50	**15.** 68
16. 69	**17.** 93	**18.** 88		

Problem Set C

1. 329	**2.** 479	**3.** 578	**4.** 799	**5.** 796
6. 785	**7.** 599	**8.** 348	**9.** 948	**10.** 886
11. 686	**12.** 987	**13.** 787	**14.** 789	**15.** 888

Subtracting Single-, Double-, and Triple-Digit Numbers

Back in the first grade your child worked out many subtraction problems. In Minilessons 51 and 52, we'll be doing still more subtraction of single- and double-digit numbers. These minilessons will be part review and part new work. In Minilesson 53 we'll tackle the subtraction of triple-digit numbers.

MINILESSON 51

Subtracting Single-Digit Numbers

We're going to take our subtraction problems a step further. In the first grade, your child subtracted single-digit numbers from other single-digit numbers. For example, $9 - 5 = 4$. Now we'll be subtracting single-digit numbers from double-digit numbers.

Ask your child to subtract 8 from 19.

$$\begin{array}{r} 19 \\ -\ 8 \\ \hline \end{array} \qquad Answer: \begin{array}{r} 19 \\ -\ 8 \\ \hline 11 \end{array}$$

What we did here was to subtract 8 from 9, which gave us 1, and then subtracted 0 from 1 to get 1. The 0 was understood. We could have written the problem this way:

$$\begin{array}{r} 19 \\ -08 \\ \hline 11 \end{array}$$

Here's another problem to work out:

$$\begin{array}{r} 14 \\ -\ 2 \\ \hline \end{array}$$ *Answer:* $$\begin{array}{r} 14 \\ -\ 2 \\ \hline 12 \end{array}$$

The problem could have been written this way:

$$\begin{array}{r} 14 \\ -02 \\ \hline 12 \end{array}$$

By convention, we don't place the 0 before the 2, as we did here. So from now on, the 0 will be understood but not actually written.

Now have your child try a whole set of these problems:

Problem Set A

1. $\begin{array}{r}18\\-\ 7\\\hline\end{array}$	**2.** $\begin{array}{r}16\\-\ 6\\\hline\end{array}$	**3.** $\begin{array}{r}19\\-\ 3\\\hline\end{array}$	**4.** $\begin{array}{r}15\\-\ 4\\\hline\end{array}$	**5.** $\begin{array}{r}12\\-\ 2\\\hline\end{array}$
6. $\begin{array}{r}14\\-\ 3\\\hline\end{array}$	**7.** $\begin{array}{r}17\\-\ 6\\\hline\end{array}$	**8.** $\begin{array}{r}16\\-\ 4\\\hline\end{array}$	**9.** $\begin{array}{r}11\\-\ 0\\\hline\end{array}$	**10.** $\begin{array}{r}18\\-\ 8\\\hline\end{array}$
11. $\begin{array}{r}15\\-\ 3\\\hline\end{array}$	**12.** $\begin{array}{r}19\\-\ 5\\\hline\end{array}$	**13.** $\begin{array}{r}14\\-\ 4\\\hline\end{array}$	**14.** $\begin{array}{r}13\\-\ 2\\\hline\end{array}$	**15.** $\begin{array}{r}18\\-\ 6\\\hline\end{array}$

Answers on page 169.

MINILESSON 52

Subtracting Double-Digit Numbers

This minilesson is basically a review of double-digit subtraction already covered in the first grade. This review sets up the next set of subtraction minilessons, when we carry subtraction a step further.

Let's work out this problem:

$$\begin{array}{r} 87 \\ -43 \\ \hline \end{array}$$

$$Answer: \quad \begin{array}{r} 87 \\ -43 \\ \hline 44 \end{array}$$

As you can see, double-digit subtraction is the same process as single-digit subtraction. Here, instead of subtracting one number from another, we subtract two numbers from two other numbers.

Now try Problem Set B.

Problem Set B				
1. $\begin{array}{r} 34 \\ -13 \\ \hline \end{array}$	**2.** $\begin{array}{r} 68 \\ -56 \\ \hline \end{array}$	**3.** $\begin{array}{r} 25 \\ -11 \\ \hline \end{array}$	**4.** $\begin{array}{r} 46 \\ -24 \\ \hline \end{array}$	**5.** $\begin{array}{r} 73 \\ -21 \\ \hline \end{array}$
6. $\begin{array}{r} 57 \\ -31 \\ \hline \end{array}$	**7.** $\begin{array}{r} 84 \\ -32 \\ \hline \end{array}$	**8.** $\begin{array}{r} 53 \\ -22 \\ \hline \end{array}$	**9.** $\begin{array}{r} 18 \\ -14 \\ \hline \end{array}$	**10.** $\begin{array}{r} 64 \\ -23 \\ \hline \end{array}$
11. $\begin{array}{r} 90 \\ -70 \\ \hline \end{array}$	**12.** $\begin{array}{r} 75 \\ -40 \\ \hline \end{array}$	**13.** $\begin{array}{r} 17 \\ -10 \\ \hline \end{array}$	**14.** $\begin{array}{r} 49 \\ -37 \\ \hline \end{array}$	**15.** $\begin{array}{r} 76 \\ -53 \\ \hline \end{array}$
16. $\begin{array}{r} 82 \\ -11 \\ \hline \end{array}$	**17.** $\begin{array}{r} 61 \\ -10 \\ \hline \end{array}$	**18.** $\begin{array}{r} 29 \\ -17 \\ \hline \end{array}$		

Answers on page 169.

Subtracting Triple-Digit Numbers

Let's get right into it by doing this problem:

$$
\begin{array}{r}
236 \\
-124 \\
\end{array}
$$

Answer:
$$
\begin{array}{r}
236 \\
-124 \\
\hline
112 \\
\end{array}
$$

Let's do one more practice problem:

$$
\begin{array}{r}
547 \\
-346 \\
\end{array}
$$

Answer:
$$
\begin{array}{r}
547 \\
-346 \\
\hline
201 \\
\end{array}
$$

Now I think we're ready for a problem set.

Problem Set C

1. 196 −175	**2.** 734 −524	**3.** 650 −410	**4.** 807 −405	**5.** 968 −707
6. 593 −391	**7.** 846 −725	**8.** 652 −622	**9.** 368 −255	**10.** 590 −390
11. 838 −736	**12.** 659 −604	**13.** 814 −404	**14.** 322 −102	**15.** 287 −270

Answers on page 169.

Triple-digit subtraction is done just the way double-digit subtraction is done. It's easy to do as long as the top digits are larger than the bottom digits. Later on, in Chapter 24, we'll be doing subtraction problems in which some of the bottom digits will be larger than the top digits.

Answers to Chapter 20 Problem Sets

Problem Set A

1. 11	**2.** 10	**3.** 16	**4.** 11	**5.** 10
6. 11	**7.** 11	**8.** 12	**9.** 11	**10.** 10
11. 12	**12.** 14	**13.** 10	**14.** 11	**15.** 12

Problem Set B

1. 21	**2.** 12	**3.** 14	**4.** 22	**5.** 52
6. 26	**7.** 52	**8.** 31	**9.** 4	**10.** 41
11. 20	**12.** 35	**13.** 7	**14.** 12	**15.** 23
16. 71	**17.** 51	**18.** 12		

Problem Set C

1. 21	**2.** 210	**3.** 240	**4.** 402	**5.** 261
6. 202	**7.** 121	**8.** 30	**9.** 113	**10.** 200
11. 102	**12.** 55	**13.** 410	**14.** 220	**15.** 17

Chapter 21

Word Problems in Addition and Subtraction

Back in the first grade we introduced word problems. In Minilesson 54 we'll do some word problems calling for addition, and in Minilesson 55 some problems calling for subtraction.

MINILESSON 54

Word Problems in Addition

These problems call for adding two, three, or four numbers. To do each problem, write an equation and solve it. Here's one example:

> Misha has four potatoes, Svetlana has five potatoes, and Ivan has three potatoes. How many potatoes do they have in all?

Answer: $4 + 5 = 9$; $9 + 3 = 12$

Now do all the problems in Problem Set A.

Problem Set A

1. Melissa had four seashells. She found six more. How many seashells does she now have?

2. The San Francisco Forty-Niners scored 21 points in the second half of their game against the Los Angeles Rams. If the Rams scored 17 points, how many points were scored by both teams in the second half?

3. How much is 2 plus 3 plus 4 plus 5?

4. Ms. O'Connor has 12 aunts and uncles and Mr. Olson has 16 aunts and uncles. How many aunts and uncles do they have altogether?

5. Jason caught five fish, Peggy caught three, and their mother caught six. How many fish did they catch altogether?

6. Carlos has five blue books, three red books, and six green books. How many books does Carlos have?

7. Start with the number 3. Add 4 to it. Then add 2 more. And then add 6. How much do you have?

8. Start with the number 4. Add 5 to it. Then add 3 more. And then add 6. How much do you have?

9. Add two, five, one, and six.

10. Mr. Ching had 8 dollars. Mrs. Veloso had 6 dollars, and Ms. Schmidt had 5 dollars. How much money did the three of them have?

11. In the meadow Roberto saw two white horses, five black horses, and nine gray horses. How many horses did he see in all?

12. Marlene had four marbles. Jerry gave her five more. Then Stu gave her another seven. How many marbles did Marlene have altogether?

13. There were six chairs in the classroom. Mrs. Jackson placed five more chairs in the room. Then Mr. Ruiz placed another six in the room. Altogether, how many chairs were there in the room?

Answers on page 173.

MINILESSON 55

Word Problems in Subtraction

This minilesson is very much like the last one, except that now we'll be subtracting instead of adding.

Try this problem:

> Yuri had 13 lollipops. He gave four to Kimberly and three to Diane. How many lollipops did he have left?

Answer: $13 - 4 = 9$; $9 - 3 = 6$

Now do Problem Set B.

Problem Set B

1. Lisa had seven balloons. She broke six of them. How many balloons does she have left?

2. Sam had 12 baseballs for sale. He sold seven of them. How many baseballs does he have left?

3. Jessica had 19 pennies. She gave four to Alan and seven to Sue Ann. How many pennies does she have left?

4. Isabel had 18 bracelets. She gave six to Alice and seven to Elena. How many bracelets did she have left?

5. Barbara began the day with 19 pieces of candy. She ate four pieces after breakfast, three after lunch, and two after supper. How many pieces of candy did she have left at the end of the day?

6. Wei had 34 marbles. He gave 21 to José. How many marbles does Wei have left?

7. How much is 65 minus 32?

8. How much is 46 take away 33?

9. Start with the number 17. Subtract 3 from it. Then subtract 2. And then subtract 7. How much do you have left?

10. Mr. Kawaguchi owned an apartment house with 43 vacant apartments. If he rented out eight apartments last week and five more this week, how many apartments are still vacant?

11. Harvey Cohen had 47 clean shirts two weeks ago. He wore six shirts a week ago and five shirts this week. How many clean shirts does he have left?

Answers below.

Answers to Chapter 21 Problem Sets

Problem Set A

1. $4 + 6 = 10$

2. $21 + 17 = 38$

3. $2 + 3 = 5$; $5 + 4 = 9$; $9 + 5 = 14$

4. $12 + 16 = 28$

5. $5 + 3 = 8$; $8 + 6 = 14$

6. $5 + 3 = 8$; $8 + 6 = 14$

7. $3 + 4 = 7$; $7 + 2 = 9$; $9 + 6 = 15$

8. $4 + 5 = 9$; $9 + 3 = 12$; $12 + 6 = 18$

9. $2 + 5 = 7$; $7 + 1 = 8$; $8 + 6 = 14$

10. $8 + 6 = 14$; $14 + 5 = 19$

11. $2 + 5 = 7$; $7 + 9 = 16$

12. $4 + 5 = 9$; $9 + 5 = 14$; $14 + 7 = 21$

13. $6 + 5 = 11$; $11 + 6 = 17$

Problem Set B

1. $7 - 6 = 1$

2. $12 - 7 = 5$

3. $19 - 4 = 15$; $15 - 7 = 8$

4. $18 - 6 = 12$; $12 - 7 = 5$

5. $19 - 4 = 15$; $15 - 3 = 12$; $12 - 2 = 10$

6. $34 - 21 = 13$

7. $65 - 32 = 33$

8. $46 - 33 = 13$

9. $17 - 3 = 14$; $14 - 2 = 12$; $12 - 7 = 5$

10. $43 - 8 = 35$; $35 - 5 = 30$

11. $47 - 6 = 41$; $41 - 5 = 36$

Regrouping, Expanded Notation, and Graphing

Your child is definitely going to need your help for Minilessons 56 and 57. You'll probably have to go over everything step by step. This is a large part of the "new math," so some of this may be new not only to your child but to you as well.

All we're really doing is regrouping each number into 100s, 10s, and 1s. For example, the number 463 has four 100s, six 10s, and three 1s. That's all there is to it.

Why do we want to regroup? There are two reasons. First, regrouping helps your child understand that a number like 729 is made up of seven 100s, two 10s, and nine 1s. There is a greater emphasis today than there was 20 or 30 years ago on understanding mathematical concepts rather than just finding the right answers. And second, regrouping provides an alternative method of adding numbers, which your child will need to master. We'll be using that alternative method in Minilesson 56.

Your child will need your help getting started in Minilesson 56, where we take up regrouping, and in Minilesson 57, when regrouping is done on graph paper. You'll need about a dozen sheets of graph paper for this chapter.

MINILESSON 56

Regrouping and Expanded Notation

Regrouping

To help understand addition, you can regroup numbers into 10s and 1s like this:

$$23 = 20 + 3$$
$$+34 = 30 + 4$$
$$57 \quad\quad 50 + 7 = 57$$

You can also regroup higher numbers into 100s, 10s, and 1s, like this:

$$235 = 200 + 30 + 5$$
$$+153 = 100 + 50 + 3$$
$$388 \quad\quad 300 + 80 + 8 = 388$$

Here's a problem to work out. First regroup and then add these two numbers:

$$45$$
$$+32$$

Solution:

$$45 = 40 + 5$$
$$+32 = 30 + 2$$
$$70 + 7 = 77$$

If you got that one right, try this one:

$$214$$
$$+575$$

Solution:

$$214 = 200 + 10 + 4$$
$$+575 = 500 + 70 + 5$$
$$700 + 80 + 9 = 789$$

Are you ready for a set of problems? All right, then, here we go.

Problem Set A

Regroup and then add the numbers in these problems.

1.	17 +25	**2.**	36 +43

3. 51
+46

4. 134
+355

5. 142
+457

6. 503
+495

Answers on pages 185–186.

Expanded Notation

Regrouping results in expanded notation. If we regrouped the number 35, it would result in an expanded notation of 30 + 5.

Right now the terms regrouping and expanded notation can be used interchangeably, but by the end of fourth grade, expanded notation will be expressed in additional ways. Regrouping enables us to use expanded notation for simple addition. Right now let's start by regrouping the numbers 24 and 47.

$$24 \quad = \quad 20 \quad + \quad 4$$

$$47 \quad = \quad 40 \quad + \quad 7$$

Now suppose we wanted to add 24 and 47 first using regrouping and then expanded notation. Here's how we'd do it:

$$
\begin{array}{rcrcr}
24 & = & 20 & + & 4 \\
+47 & = & 40 & + & 7 \\
\hline
 & & 60 & + & 11 \quad = 60 + 10 + 1 = 70 + 1 = 71
\end{array}
$$

Try adding these two numbers by means of regrouping and expanded notation:

56
+39

Answer:

56	=	50	+	6
+39	=	30	+	9
		80	+	15 = 80 + 10 + 5 = 90 + 5 = 95

What we're doing is adding tens and then adding ones. So we start here with 80 + 15, and regroup 15 into 10 + 5. Then we add 80 + 10 and get 90. And 90 + 5 = 95.

Here's a problem set to provide you with more practice.

Problem Set B

Regroup in expanded notation and add each of these sets of numbers.

1. 37
  +25

2. 28
  +46

3. 55
  +39

Answers on page 186.

As a parent, you may wonder what the point of all of this is. Regrouping and expanded notation are part of the "new math." Its purpose is to have your child understand that numbers are made up of 1s, (or units), 10s, 100s, and still larger denominations. If your child seems confused about this, work through the following Extra Help box with her.

Regrouping and Expanded Notation

First, have your child regroup these numbers:

$$37$$
$$\underline{+56}$$

Answer:

37	=	30	+	7
+56	=	50	+	6

The next step is to add these numbers using expanded notation. Let's see if your child can do that.

Answer:

37	=	30	+	7
+56	=	50	+	6
	=	80	+	13 = 80 + 10 + 3 = 90 + 3 = 93

And now have your child regroup these numbers and then add them using expanded notation:

$$28$$
$$\underline{+49}$$

Answer:

28	=	20	+	8
+49	=	40	+	9
		60	+	17 = 60 + 10 + 7 = 70 + 7 = 77

If your child now understands how to use expanded notation, go directly to Minilesson 57. If not, make up your own problems and have him keep working out the answers until he consistently gets them right.

MINILESSON 57

Graphing 100s, 10s, and 1s

In the previous minilesson your child regrouped numbers into 100s, 10s, and 1s. For example, 238 can be regrouped as 200 + 30 + 8. Here we'll be representing the number 238 in terms of boxes.

The graph below shows the number 238 as a series of boxes. The purpose here is again to help your child understand what numbers really mean. Each box on the graph represents the number 1. Ten boxes represent 10, and 100 boxes represent 100.

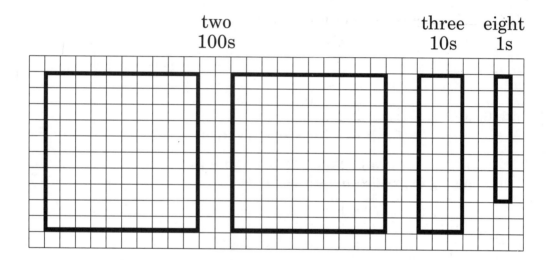

The large box to the left is made up of 100 boxes. The large box right next to it is also made up of 100 boxes. Since 100 + 100 = 200, these two large boxes are our two sets of 100. Next come the 10s. Moving to the right, the box that is 10 lines high and 3 lines across is made up of 30 boxes, or three lines of boxes of 10 each. These 30 boxes represent 30. And finally, all the way over to the right, there are eight boxes, which represent the eight 1s in 238.

See if your child can regroup the number 457. Did he get 400 + 50 + 7? Good!

Now have him use the blank graph paper below to put the 100s, 10, and 1s in boxes.

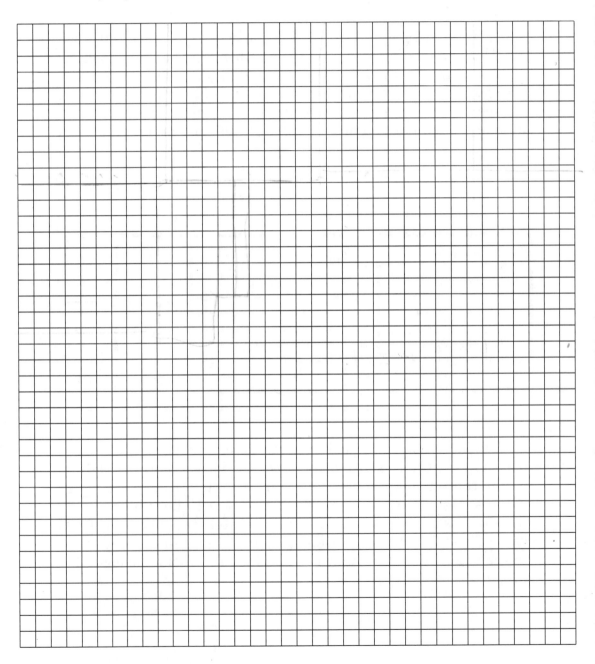

Did his chart look something like the one below?

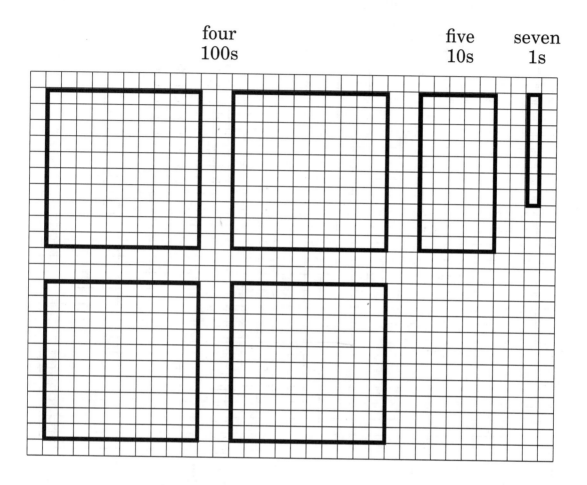

four
100s

five
10s

seven
1s

Now have your child read through and do the next few examples on his own. Let's first regroup the number 629.

Did you get 600 + 20 + 9? Now use the blank graph paper below to put the numbers into boxes.

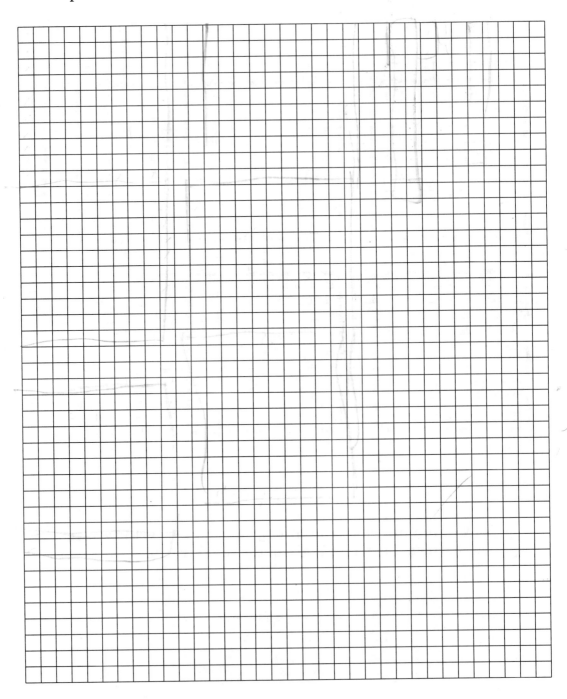

Compare your boxes to those in the graph below.

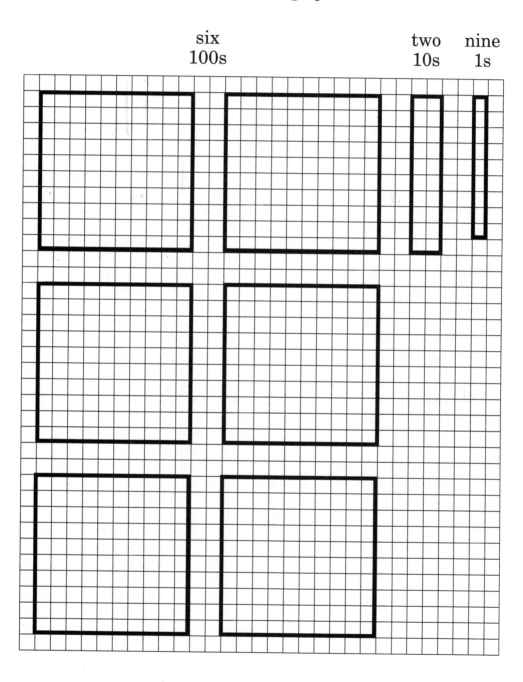

Let's try one more. First, regroup 457.

Did you get 400 + 50 + 7? Now use the blank graph paper below to put these 100s, 10s, and 1s into boxes.

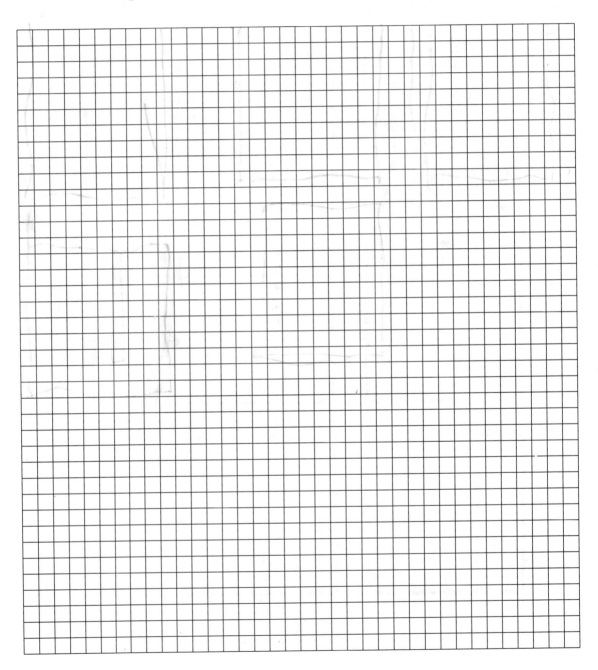

Make sure that your boxes look like the ones in this graph:

four
100s

five
10s

seven
1s

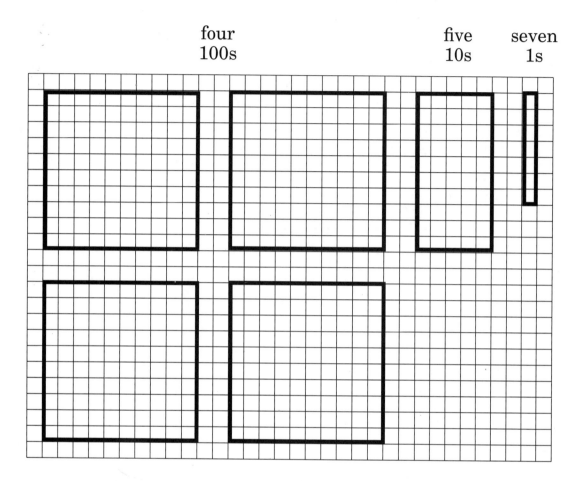

Answers to Chapter 22 Problem Sets

Problem Set A

1.   17 = 10 + 7
     +25 = 20 + 5
           30 + 12 = 42

2.   36 = 30 + 6
     +43 = 40 + 3
           70 + 9 = 79

3.   51 = 50 + 1
     +46 = 40 + 6
           90 + 7 = 97

4.   134 = 100 + 30 + 4
     +355 = 300 + 50 + 5
            400 + 80 + 9 = 489

5. $142 =$ $100 + 40 + 2$
$\underline{+457} =$ $\underline{400 + 50 + 7}$
$500 + 90 + 9 = 599$

6. $503 =$ $500 + 0 + 3$
$\underline{+495} =$ $\underline{400 + 90 + 5}$
$900 + 90 + 8 = 998$

Problem Set B

1. $37 = 30 + 7$
$\underline{+25} = \underline{20 + 5}$
$50 + 12 = 50 + 10 + 2 = 60 + 2 = 62$

2. $28 = 20 + 8$
$\underline{+46} = \underline{40 + 6}$
$60 + 14 = 60 + 10 + 4 = 70 + 4 = 74$

3. $55 = 50 + 5$
$\underline{+39} = \underline{30 + 9}$
$80 + 14 = 80 + 10 + 4 = 90 + 4 = 94$

Addition with Carrying

We now begin addition with carrying. In Minilesson 58, we'll be adding two one-digit numbers. Then, over the course of the next four minilessons, we'll work our way up to adding three two-digit numbers.

Adding Two Single-Digit Numbers with Carrying

If you ask your child to add 9 + 3, there are two ways she can do it. One way is to count three up from 9: 10, 11, 12. The other way is to carry.

Carrying works like this:

$$
\begin{array}{r} 9 \\ +3 \\ \hline \end{array}
\qquad
\text{Since } 9 + 3 = 12, \text{ we put down 2 under the 3 and carry the one 10:}
\qquad
\begin{array}{r} \overset{1}{9} \\ +3 \\ \hline 2 \end{array}
\qquad
\text{Then bring down the 10:}
\qquad
\begin{array}{r} \overset{1}{9} \\ +3 \\ \hline 12 \end{array}
$$

If your child understands this, have her read through the rest of the minilesson on her own.

Try this problem using carrying:

7 + 8 = ?

$$
\textit{Answer:}\quad
\begin{array}{r} \overset{1}{7} \\ +8 \\ \hline 15 \end{array}
$$

Now try this set of problems. Remember to carry, even if you know the answer without carrying.

Problem Set A

1. 6 +8	**2.** 9 +5	**3.** 5 +6	**4.** 8 +4	**5.** 9 +7	**6.** 6 +4
7. 3 +8	**8.** 7 +5	**9.** 8 +9	**10.** 5 +8	**11.** 1 +9	**12.** 8 +2
13. 9 +6	**14.** 8 +8	**15.** 6 +7	**16.** 9 +9	**17.** 7 +7	**18.** 6 +6

Answers on page 197.

MINILESSON 59

Adding Two Double-Digit Numbers with Carrying

In order to add properly, your child needs to know two basic things: (1) the addition table; and (2) carrying. We covered the addition table in Minilessons 6, 7, and 17 in first-grade math, near the beginning of the book. And we introduced carrying in the previous minilesson. Here carrying will get trickier. Keep working together until she has successfully done all the problems in this set. Sometimes still more practice is needed. That practice is provided in the next minilesson.

Let's apply to double-digit numbers what we've learned about addition and carrying. Go through this problem with your child.

$$57$$
$$+39$$

We add the 7 to the 9 and get 16, so we write down the 6 under the 9 and carry the one 10, like this→

$$\begin{array}{r} 1 \\ 57 \\ +39 \\ \hline 6 \end{array}$$

Then we add the one 10 to the five 10s and three 10s (1 + 5 + 3) and get nine 10s.

$$\begin{array}{r} 1 \\ 57 \\ +39 \\ \hline 96 \end{array}$$

If your child understands this, have her do the rest of the minilesson on her own, but check her work when she's finished. If she gets more than one problem wrong in the last problem set, you should sit down with her and go over each sample problem and each problem in the problem set. Have her work out the first one with you. Ask her to tell you what she's doing as she does it. After you've worked out the first problem together, move on to the next and go through the whole problem set.

$$\begin{array}{r} 44 \\ +38 \\ \hline \end{array}$$

Solution:

$$\begin{array}{r} 1 \\ 44 \\ +38 \\ \hline 82 \end{array}$$

Since this can seem complicated when you first try it, we'll go over a few more together.

Try adding these numbers, remembering to carry.

$$\begin{array}{r} 17 \\ +19 \\ \hline \end{array}$$

What did you get? If you got 36, you're right! Let's go over the problem step by step.

We add the 7 to the 9 and get 16. So we write down the 6 under the 9 and carry the one 10, like this→

$$\begin{array}{r} 1 \\ 17 \\ +19 \\ \hline 6 \end{array}$$

To make sure we don't forget to carry the 10, we write a tiny 1 to represent one 10 just above the 1 of the 17. Next we add that tiny 1 to the one 10 of 17 and the one 10 of 19 and get three 10s. We put the 3 next to the 6, like this→

$$\begin{array}{r} 1 \\ 17 \\ +19 \\ \hline 36 \end{array}$$

That gives us 36.

Now work out the problem below, and write your answer in the space.

$$\begin{array}{r} 24 \\ +68 \\ \hline \end{array}$$

What did you get? Was your answer 92? Here it is worked out:

$$\begin{array}{r} 1 \\ 24 \\ +68 \\ \hline 92 \end{array}$$

Problem Set B

1. $\begin{array}{r} 22 \\ +49 \\ \hline \end{array}$ **2.** $\begin{array}{r} 61 \\ +19 \\ \hline \end{array}$ **3.** $\begin{array}{r} 37 \\ +46 \\ \hline \end{array}$ **4.** $\begin{array}{r} 29 \\ +45 \\ \hline \end{array}$ **5.** $\begin{array}{r} 72 \\ +19 \\ \hline \end{array}$

6. $\begin{array}{r} 48 \\ +27 \\ \hline \end{array}$ **7.** $\begin{array}{r} 49 \\ +49 \\ \hline \end{array}$ **8.** $\begin{array}{r} 57 \\ +13 \\ \hline \end{array}$ **9.** $\begin{array}{r} 79 \\ +14 \\ \hline \end{array}$ **10.** $\begin{array}{r} 54 \\ +18 \\ \hline \end{array}$

11. $\begin{array}{r} 68 \\ +19 \\ \hline \end{array}$ **12.** $\begin{array}{r} 46 \\ +36 \\ \hline \end{array}$ **13.** $\begin{array}{r} 53 \\ +37 \\ \hline \end{array}$ **14.** $\begin{array}{r} 67 \\ +29 \\ \hline \end{array}$ **15.** $\begin{array}{r} 24 \\ +38 \\ \hline \end{array}$

Answers on page 197.

That was so much fun, let's do another set of problems:

Problem Set C

1. 24 +39	**2.** 16 +15	**3.** 37 +48	**4.** 25 +49	**5.** 58 +36
6. 47 +3	**7.** 29 +36	**8.** 65 +25	**9.** 74 +17	**10.** 68 +27
11. 56 +15	**12.** 29 +49	**13.** 72 +18	**14.** 45 +19	**15.** 58 +26

Answers on page 197.

Now make up your own problems. After you have finished them, show them to your parents to see if they can solve the problems you made up.

MINILESSON 60

Adding Three Single-Digit Numbers with Carrying

In Minilesson 17 your child added two single-digit numbers using carrying. Then in Minilesson 25 we added two double-digit numbers. What comes next? Adding three single-digit numbers comes next.

Ask your child to do this problem:

$$
\begin{array}{r}
5 \\
8 \\
+7 \\
\hline
\end{array}
$$

If he got 20, then he can go directly to Problem Set D. If not, you'll need to go over the problem with him. Ask him to add 5 and 8. He should get 13. Then ask him to add 13 and 7. These add to 20.

Now ask him to do this problem:

$$
\begin{array}{r}
9 \\
7 \\
+6 \\
\hline
\end{array}
$$

If he got 22, then go directly to Problem Set D. If he got this wrong, ask him to add 9 + 7. He should get 16. Then ask him to add 16 + 6. They add up to 22.

If he got both problems wrong, turn back to the beginning of this chapter and have him repeat Minilessons 58 and 59, and then redo this minilesson as well. Addition with carrying has got to be mastered before he can proceed to adding three single-digit numbers.

Now do Problem Set D.

Problem Set D

1. 8 4 +9	**2.** 6 9 +6	**3.** 8 7 +6	**4.** 9 5 +6	**5.** 7 9 +4	**6.** 9 5 +8
7. 9 9 +8	**8.** 8 7 +5	**9.** 7 8 +9	**10.** 6 8 +9	**11.** 8 8 +4	**12.** 5 8 +8
13. 6 6 +9	**14.** 7 9 +9	**15.** 9 4 +8	**16.** 6 9 +8	**17.** 8 9 +5	**18.** 9 9 +9

Answers on page 197.

MINILESSON 61

Adding Three Double-Digit Numbers with Carrying

Carrying is one of the most important concepts covered in this book. When your child gets it down, she will find that math will be not only easier but a lot more fun. If your child runs into difficulty, review Minilessons 48 through 50. Now we're going to try something a little harder. We're going to add three double-digit numbers. Do the first one together.

Try to add:

$$
\begin{array}{r}
15 \\
12 \\
+22 \\
\hline
\end{array}
$$

The process is a combination of adding three single-digit numbers and adding two double-digit numbers. Or adding three single-digit numbers twice. As long as you know how to carry, you're in business. We work this problem out like this:

5 + 2 + 2 = 9, so we put the 9 under these numbers:

$$
\begin{array}{r}
15 \\
12 \\
+22 \\
\hline
9 \\
\end{array}
$$

Then we add the 10s: one 10 + one 10 + two 10s, = four 10s, so we put the four 10s next to the 9:

$$
\begin{array}{r}
15 \\
12 \\
+22 \\
\hline
49 \\
\end{array}
$$

If your child understood that, have her do the rest of the minilesson on her own. But encourage her to ask for help if she needs it, and be sure to check her answers when she's done. Now do this problem:

$$
\begin{array}{r}
32 \\
21 \\
13 \\
\hline
\end{array}
$$

Did you get 66? Good. You'll notice that I didn't bother putting plus signs (+). Why not? Because in mathematics, if there are three or more numbers listed and a line under the bottom number, it is understood that you are going to add the numbers unless there is another sign there.

Here's another one to try:

$$\begin{array}{r} 43 \\ 17 \\ \underline{15} \end{array}$$

This problem requires carrying. When we add 3 + 7 + 5, we get 15. So we put down the 5 and carry the one 10 to the top of the next column.

$$\begin{array}{r} 1 \\ 43 \\ 17 \\ \underline{15} \\ 5 \end{array}$$

Then we continue with the problem by adding the tiny one 10 + four 10s + one 10 + one 10 to get seven 10s. If you put the seven 10s next to the 5, that gives us an answer of 75.

$$\begin{array}{r} 1 \\ 43 \\ 17 \\ \underline{15} \\ 75 \end{array}$$

Now do the following problem set.

Problem Set E

1. 11 17 $\underline{14}$	**2.** 10 12 $\underline{18}$	**3.** 14 19 $\underline{16}$	**4.** 18 16 $\underline{12}$	**5.** 15 18 $\underline{17}$	**6.** 19 20 $\underline{24}$
7. 26 17 $\underline{14}$	**8.** 25 21 $\underline{18}$	**9.** 29 24 $\underline{20}$	**10.** 10 22 $\underline{19}$	**11.** 15 26 $\underline{29}$	**12.** 18 24 $\underline{21}$

13. 31
27
<u>24</u>

14. 28
36
<u>23</u>

15. 17
34
<u>28</u>

16. 22
27
<u>36</u>

17. 33
29
<u>14</u>

18. 42
16
<u>13</u>

Answers on page 197.

Problem Set F

1. 11
24
<u>52</u>

2. 14
23
<u>40</u>

3. 51
10
<u>36</u>

4. 15
42
<u>32</u>

5. 64
21
<u>13</u>

6. 25
34
<u>20</u>

7. 16
19
<u>14</u>

8. 25
34
<u>40</u>

9. 29
22
<u>38</u>

10. 17
15
<u>44</u>

11. 45
27
<u>16</u>

12. 16
37
<u>45</u>

13. 53
28
<u>16</u>

14. 38
29
<u>12</u>

15. 56
30
<u>9</u>

Answers on page 197.

When you've finished, check your work and ask your parent to check it, too.

MINILESSON 62

Summary of Addition with Carrying

We saved the best for last. So far your child has added two single-digit numbers, then two double-digit numbers, and then three single-digit numbers. And after that he added three double-digit numbers.

Now we're going to put all these problems together in one final set of problems. So while we won't be covering any new material, your child will get to do several different types of problems in the same problem set. Ask him to try the problem set on his own. If he has difficulty, review Minilessons 58 through 61.

Problem Set G

1. 9
  +7
	2. 23
	  +38
		3. 9
		  8
		  5
			4. 17
			  15
			  12
				5. 34
				  10
				  18

6. 19
  5
  12
	7. 24
	  +58
		8. 9
		  8
		  8
			9. 16
			  12
			  7
				10. 32
				  29
				  16

11. 46
  +38
	12. 10
	  17
	  15
		13. 8
		  8
		  7
			14. 29
			  27
			  24
				15. 58
				  +29

16. 23
  16
  8
	17. 6
	  8
	  9
		18. 38
		  27
		  18
			19. 12
			  46
			  29
				20. 6
				  19
				  26

Answers on page 197.

Answers to Chapter 23 Problem Sets

Problem Set A

1. 14	**2.** 14	**3.** 11	**4.** 12	**5.** 16	**6.** 10
7. 11	**8.** 12	**9.** 17	**10.** 13	**11.** 10	**12.** 10
13. 15	**14.** 16	**15.** 13	**16.** 18	**17.** 14	**18.** 12

Problem Set B

1. 71	**2.** 80	**3.** 83	**4.** 74	**5.** 91
6. 75	**7.** 98	**8.** 70	**9.** 93	**10.** 72
11. 87	**12.** 82	**13.** 90	**14.** 96	**15.** 62

Problem Set C

1. 63	**2.** 31	**3.** 85	**4.** 74	**5.** 94
6. 50	**7.** 65	**8.** 90	**9.** 91	**10.** 95
11. 71	**12.** 78	**13.** 90	**14.** 64	**15.** 84

Problem Set D

1. 21	**2.** 21	**3.** 21	**4.** 20	**5.** 20	**6.** 22
7. 26	**8.** 20	**9.** 24	**10.** 23	**11.** 20	**12.** 21
13. 21	**14.** 25	**15.** 21	**16.** 23	**17.** 22	**18.** 27

Problem Set E

1. 42	**2.** 40	**3.** 49	**4.** 46	**5.** 50	**6.** 63
7. 57	**8.** 64	**9.** 73	**10.** 51	**11.** 70	**12.** 63
13. 82	**14.** 87	**15.** 79	**16.** 85	**17.** 76	**18.** 71

Problem Set F

1. 87	**2.** 77	**3.** 97	**4.** 89	**5.** 98
6. 79	**7.** 49	**8.** 99	**9.** 89	**10.** 76
11. 88	**12.** 98	**13.** 97	**14.** 79	**15.** 95

Problem Set G

1. 16	**2.** 61	**3.** 22	**4.** 44	**5.** 62
6. 36	**7.** 82	**8.** 25	**9.** 35	**10.** 77
11. 84	**12.** 42	**13.** 23	**14.** 80	**15.** 87
16. 47	**17.** 23	**18.** 83	**19.** 87	**20.** 51

Subtraction with Borrowing and Review of Carrying and Borrowing

In Minilesson 63 we'll go over subtraction with borrowing step by step. Once your child learns to borrow, he'll have no trouble doing even the most difficult subtraction problem. Minilesson 64 is a quiz to check how well he has learned carrying and borrowing.

Subtraction with Borrowing

Explain to your child that borrowing is something like carrying. We use it in subtraction when the digit we are taking away is larger than the digit we are taking it from.

Work out this first borrowing problem with your child →

$$\begin{array}{r} 52 \\ -38 \\ \hline \end{array}$$

The first step is to subtract 8 from 2. Since 2 is smaller than 8, we need to borrow one 10 from 52. That will increase the 2 to 12 (because 2 + 10 = 12), but it will also decrease 10s the five to four 10s. We write it like this →

$$\begin{array}{r} \overset{4}{\cancel{5}}\overset{1}{2} \\ -38 \\ \hline \end{array}$$

Now we can carry out the subtraction by first subtracting 12 − 8 to get 4. Write the 4 under the 8, like this →

$$\begin{array}{r} \overset{4}{\cancel{5}}\overset{1}{2} \\ -38 \\ \hline 4 \end{array}$$

Then subtract four 10s − three 10s to get one 10. Write the 1, which represents one 10, next to the 4 to get 14.

$$\begin{array}{r} \overset{4}{\cancel{5}}\overset{1}{2} \\ -38 \\ \hline 14 \end{array}$$

Here's another problem for you to do with
your child →

$$\begin{array}{r} 65 \\ -28 \\ \hline \end{array}$$

First we subtract 8 from 5. Since 5 is smaller
than 8, we need to borrow one 10 from 65. That
will increase 5 to 15, but it will also decrease
the six 10s to five 10s →

$$\begin{array}{r} {}^{5}{}^{1}5 \\ \cancel{6}5 \\ -28 \\ \hline \end{array}$$

Now we subtract 8 from 15 to get 7, and write
the 7 under the 8, like this →

$$\begin{array}{r} {}^{5}{}^{1}5 \\ \cancel{6}5 \\ -28 \\ \hline 7 \end{array}$$

Then subtract five 10s – two 10s to get three
10s. Write the 3, which represents three 10s,
next to the 7 to get 37.

$$\begin{array}{r} {}^{5}{}^{1}5 \\ \cancel{6}5 \\ -28 \\ \hline 37 \end{array}$$

Let your child go on from here by himself.

If you understand those, do Problem Sets A and B. If you need
more help, read the Extra Help box with your parent.

EXTRA HELP

Subtraction with Borrowing

Ask your child to do this problem →

$$\begin{array}{r} 72 \\ -39 \\ \hline \end{array}$$

If he got 33, then he's ready for Problem Set A. If not, then work
it out with him step by step:

First we subtract 9 from 2. Since 2 is smaller than 9,
we need to borrow one 10 from 72. That will increase
2 to 12, but it will also decrease the seven 10s to six 10s.

$$\begin{array}{r} {}^{6}{}^{1}2 \\ \cancel{7}2 \\ -39 \\ \hline \end{array}$$

Now we subtract 9 from 12 to get 3, and write
the 3 like this →

$$\begin{array}{r} {}^{6}{}^{1}2 \\ \cancel{7}2 \\ -39 \\ \hline 3 \end{array}$$

$$\begin{array}{r} \overset{6}{\cancel{7}}\overset{1}{2} \\ -3\,9 \\ \hline 3\,3 \end{array}$$

Then we subtract three 10s from six 10s →

Here's another problem for your child to solve →

$$\begin{array}{r} 8\,4 \\ -4\,6 \\ \hline \end{array}$$

If he got 38, then go directly to Problem Sets A and B. If not, then show him how to do it step by step:

Subtract 6 from 4. Since 4 is smaller than 6, borrow one 10 from 84. That will increase 4 to 14, but it will also decrease the eight 10s to seven 10s.

$$\begin{array}{r} \overset{7}{\cancel{8}}\overset{1}{4} \\ -4\,6 \\ \hline \end{array}$$

Now subtract 6 from 14 to get 8, and write the 8 this way →

$$\begin{array}{r} \overset{7}{\cancel{8}}\overset{1}{4} \\ -4\,6 \\ \hline 8 \end{array}$$

Then subtract four 10s from seven 10s to get three 10s.

$$\begin{array}{r} \overset{7}{\cancel{8}}\overset{1}{4} \\ -4\,6 \\ \hline 3\,8 \end{array}$$

If your child is still having trouble with borrowing, you'll need to go through this Extra Help box with him from the beginning. After you've done that, he should be ready for Problem Sets A and B.

Problem Set A

1. 46	2. 38	3. 84	4. 91	5. 95
-27	-29	-46	-56	-29

6. 42	7. 68	8. 30	9. 53	10. 86
-17	-39	-11	-29	-48

11. 98	**12.** 62	**13.** 40	**14.** 75	**15.** 44
-39	-15	-19	-36	-28

Answers on page 204.

To make sure you're on track, try the next problem set.

Problem Set B

1. 53	**2.** 90	**3.** 25	**4.** 81	**5.** 22
-17	-21	-9	-34	-3

6. 40	**7.** 76	**8.** 92	**9.** 65	**10.** 74
-13	-58	-36	-18	-37

11. 60	**12.** 58	**13.** 24	**14.** 62	**15.** 83
-34	-19	-7	-33	-24

Answers on page 204.

When we do addition, we often have to carry. And when we do subtraction, we often have to borrow. Both carrying and borrowing are very important arithmetic tools. You must know how to borrow and carry before you can learn math in the higher grades. If you need more help, read the following Extra Help box. You may want to read it even if you don't need further help. If you're sure you have borrowing down cold, ask your parent to check your work and then go on to the quiz in Minilesson 64 to double-check how well you carry and borrow.

Carrying and Borrowing

First we'll go over carrying. Try to work out
this problem →

$$\begin{array}{r} 36 \\ +16 \\ \hline \end{array}$$

Did you get 52? Let's go over it step by step. First we
add 6 + 6. That gives us 12. We write the 2 and carry
the one 10 by writing a tiny 1 just above the three 10s
in 36, like this →

$$\begin{array}{r} 1 \\ 36 \\ +16 \\ \hline 2 \end{array}$$

Now we add that tiny one 10 to the three 10s in 36
and the one 10 in 16: one 10 + three 10s + one 10 = 5.
We write the 5 next to the 2, so our answer is 52.

$$\begin{array}{r} 1 \\ 36 \\ +16 \\ \hline 52 \end{array}$$

Are you ready for another one? Try this →

$$\begin{array}{r} 45 \\ +29 \\ \hline \end{array}$$

What did you get? Was it 74? Here's how we do it:
First we add 5 + 9 and get 14. We write down the 4 and
carry the one 10, putting a tiny 1 above the 4 in 45.
Then we add that one 10 to the four 10s in 45 and the
two 10s in 29 and get seven 10s. So our answer is 74.

$$\begin{array}{r} 1 \\ 45 \\ +29 \\ \hline 74 \end{array}$$

Next we'll go over borrowing. Try to work
out this problem →

$$\begin{array}{r} 53 \\ -37 \\ \hline \end{array}$$

What's your answer? Is it 16? When we subtract 7
from 3, we need to borrow. We borrow one 10 from 53,
making it 43, while the 3 becomes 13. Now we can
carry out the subtraction, 13 − 7 = 6, and write the 6.

$$\begin{array}{r} 4\ 1 \\ \cancel{5}3 \\ -37 \\ \hline 6 \end{array}$$

Next we subtract three 10s from four 10s, which
gives us one 10. So our answer is 16.

$$\begin{array}{r} 4\ 1 \\ \cancel{5}3 \\ -37 \\ \hline 16 \end{array}$$

Next borrowing problem →

$$\begin{array}{r} 72 \\ -29 \\ \hline \end{array}$$

Did you get 43? Again, you had to borrow.
Borrow one 10 from 72 to make the 2 into 12 and the
72 into 62. Then subtract 12 − 9 to get 3. Write the 3.

$$\begin{array}{r} \overset{6}{\cancel{7}}\overset{1}{2} \\ -29 \\ \hline 3 \end{array}$$

Now subtract six 10s − two 10s to get four 10s
Write the 4 next to the 3 to get 43.

$$\begin{array}{r} \overset{6}{\cancel{7}}\overset{1}{2} \\ -29 \\ \hline 43 \end{array}$$

Let's see how much you learned. Go back to Problem Set A, do all the problems, and then do Problem Set B. After that, you'll be ready for Minilesson 64.

MINILESSON 64

Minitest: Addition with Carrying and Subtraction with Borrowing

If your child gets no more than one addition problem and one subtraction problem wrong, then she is ready to begin Chapter 25. However, if she gets more than one addition problem wrong, she will need to repeat Minilessons 58 through 62, and if she gets more than one subtraction problem wrong, she needs to repeat Minilessons 63 and 64. After reviewing these minilessons, have her repeat this minilesson, and then go on to Chapter 25.

Two of the most important topics of the second grade are addition with carrying, which was covered in Minilessons 58 through 62, and subtraction with borrowing, which we did in the two previous minilessons. So your child's progress needs to be very closely monitored.

Problem Set C

1. 22 +39	**2.** 35 +25	**3.** 19 +17	**4.** 46 +28	**5.** 81 +9	**6.** 76 +14
7. 62 +29	**8.** 44 +28	**9.** 19 +29	**10.** 36 +19	**11.** 24 +48	**12.** 67 +17
13. 31 −27	**14.** 84 −59	**15.** 77 −38	**16.** 42 −16	**17.** 38 −29	**18.** 66 −29

Answers below.

Answers to Chapter 24 Problem Sets

Problem Set A

1. 19	**2.** 9	**3.** 38	**4.** 35	**5.** 66
6. 25	**7.** 29	**8.** 19	**9.** 24	**10.** 38
11. 59	**12.** 47	**13.** 21	**14.** 39	**15.** 16

Problem Set B

1. 36	**2.** 69	**3.** 16	**4.** 47	**5.** 19
6. 27	**7.** 18	**8.** 56	**9.** 47	**10.** 37
11. 26	**12.** 39	**13.** 17	**14.** 29	**15.** 59

Problem Set C

1. 61	**2.** 60	**3.** 36	**4.** 74	**5.** 90	**6.** 90
7. 91	**8.** 72	**9.** 48	**10.** 55	**11.** 72	**12.** 84
13. 4	**14.** 25	**15.** 39	**16.** 26	**17.** 9	**18.** 37

Adding and Subtracting Money

Adding change and subtracting change is very helpful in learning how to add and subtract. If your child is having any problems working with change, this is a good place to stop for a while to go over these concepts.

Have your child try to work through the next two minilessons on her own. Check her answers. If she gets everything right, then she won't need much help right now. But if she gets a few problems wrong, then sit down with her and watch her work through each problem in Minilessons 65 and 66. If she's having trouble with the concept of money, it will probably help if you use actual change. You'll need three quarters, five dimes, five nickels, and 14 pennies.

To do math, many children—and adults—need to visualize the problem. Sometimes that means counting on their fingers, putting objects into groups of 10, or, in this case, seeing the coins right in front of them. Use whatever works.

MINILESSON 65

Adding Money

Let's review money. How much is a dime worth? You probably know that a dime is worth 10 pennies or 10 cents. How much is a quarter worth? Twenty-five cents. How many nickels in a quarter? There are five.

Fill in the missing numbers:

A penny is _____ cent.   A dime is _____ cents.

A nickel is _____ cents.   A quarter is _____ cents.

Answers:

A penny is 1 cent.   A dime is 10 cents.

A nickel is 5 cents.   A quarter is 25 cents.

Now let's do some addition. If you had a penny, a nickel, and a dime, how much money would you have altogether?

Solution: You would have 1 cent plus 5 cents plus 10 cents: $1 + 5 + 10 = 16$. So you would have 16 cents.

How much money would you have altogether if you had a dime and two quarters?

Solution:

10 cents + 25 cents + 25 cents = 60 cents

You had to carry to do this one. Did you remember how?

$$\begin{array}{r} 1 \\ 10 \\ 25 \\ \underline{25} \\ 60 \end{array}$$

Here's a set of problems to solve.

Problem Set A

Add each of these combinations of money and write down the total for each.

1.   A quarter, two dimes, and a nickel

2.   A dime, three nickels, and two pennies

3.   Four pennies, a nickel, and a quarter

4.   Three nickels, a dime, and two quarters

5.   A quarter, three dimes, a nickel, and two pennies

6.   Eight pennies, two nickels, a dime, and a quarter

7.   Two quarters, two dimes, a nickel, and five pennies

8.   Four dimes, two nickels, and twelve pennies

9.   A quarter, three dimes, four nickels, and six pennies

Answers on page 209.

MINILESSON 66

Subtracting Money

Are you ready for something a little different? We're now going to learn how to subtract with money. If you started with 50 cents and spent a dime and four pennies, how much would you have left?

Solution:

50 cents − 10 cents = 40 cents; 40 cents − 4 cents = 36 cents

Another way we could do this is to start with 50 cents, then add the dime and four pennies together and subtract their sum from 50 cents:

50 cents − (10 + 4 cents) = 50 − 14 cents = 36 cents

Here's another problem: If you started with 72 cents and spent a quarter, two dimes, and a penny, how much would you have left?

We need to make this into a subtraction problem.

We start with 72 cents. How much do we subtract from this? We have to add up the quarter, the two dimes, and the penny.

$$\begin{array}{r} 25 \\ 10 \\ 10 \\ \underline{1} \\ 46 \text{ cents} \end{array}$$

Now we're ready to subtract the 46 cents from the 72 cents. This is done by subtraction with borrowing.

$$\begin{array}{r} 72 \\ \underline{-46} \end{array}$$

$$\begin{array}{r} {}^{6}\!\!\not{7}{}^{1}2 \\ \underline{-4\,6} \\ 2\,6 \text{ cents} \end{array}$$

Now try these problem sets.

Problem Set B

1.   How much is 70 cents minus a dime and eight pennies? 52

2.   If you start with 85 cents and spend a quarter, two dimes, and a nickel, how much will you have left?

3.   Suppose you left home with 92 cents and spent two quarters, a dime, and three pennies. How much would you have left?

4.   How much is 83 cents minus a quarter, a dime, and three nickels?

5.   How much is 67 cents minus a dime, four nickels, and three pennies?

6.   If you started with 82 cents and spent a quarter, two dimes, and two nickels, what would you end up with?

7.   How much is 91 cents minus a quarter, two dimes, three nickels, and nine pennies?

8.   How much is 83 cents minus two quarters, three nickels, and fourteen pennies?

Answers on page 209.

Problem Set C

1.   How much is 75 cents minus a quarter and four pennies?

2.   Suppose you left home with 94 cents and spent one quarter, three dimes, and two nickels. How much would you have left?

3.   How much is 84 cents minus three dimes, three nickels, and eleven pennies?

4.   How much is 91 cents minus two quarters, one dime, two nickels, and seven pennies?

5.   If you started with 84 cents and spent two quarters, three nickels, and nine pennies, what would you end up with?

6.   How much is 98 cents minus one quarter, four dimes, three nickels, and fourteen pennies?

Answers below.

Once you've finished, ask your parent to check your work.

Answers to Chapter 25 Problem Sets

Problem Set A
1. 25 + 10 + 10 + 5 = 50 cents
2. 10 + 5 + 5 + 5 + 2 = 27 cents
3. 4 + 5 + 25 = 34 cents
4. 5 + 5 + 5 + 10 + 25 + 25 = 75 cents
5. 25 + 10 + 10 + 10 + 5 + 2 = 62 cents
6. 8 + 5 + 5 + 10 + 25 = 53 cents
7. 25 + 25 + 10 + 10 + 5 + 5 = 80 cents
8. 10 + 10 + 10 + 10 + 5 + 5 + 12 = 62 cents
9. 25 + 10 + 10 + 10 + 5 + 5 + 5 + 5 + 6 = 81 cents

Problem Set B
1. 70 cents − (10 + 8 cents) = 70 − 18 cents = 52 cents
2. 85 cents − (25 + 10 + 10 + 5 cents) = 85 − 50 cents = 35 cents
3. 92 cents − (25 + 25 + 10 + 3 cents) = 92 − 63 cents = 29 cents
4. 83 cents − (25 + 10 + 5 + 5 + 5 cents) = 83 − 50 cents = 33 cents
5. 67 cents − (10 + 5 + 5 + 5 + 5 + 3 cents) = 67 − 33 cents = 34 cents
6. 82 cents − (25 + 10 + 10 + 5 + 5 cents) = 82 − 55 cents = 27 cents
7. 91 cents − (25 + 10 + 10 + 5 + 5 + 5 + 9 cents) = 91 − 69 cents = 22 cents
8. 83 cents − (25 + 25 + 5 + 5 + 5 + 14 cents) = 83 − 79 cents = 4 cents

Problem Set C
1. 75 cents − (25 + 4 cents) = 75 − 29 cents = 46 cents
2. 94 cents − (25 + 10 + 10 + 10 + 5 + 5 cents) = 94 − 65 cents = 29 cents
3. 84 cents − (10 + 10 + 10 + 5 + 5 + 5 + 11 cents) = 84 − 56 cents = 28 cents
4. 91 cents − (25 + 25 + 10 + 5 + 5 + 7 cents) = 91 − 77 cents = 14 cents
5. 84 cents − (25 + 25 + 5 + 5 + 5 + 9 cents) = 84 − 74 cents = 10 cents
6. 98 cents − (25 + 10 + 10 + 10 + 10 + 5 + 5 + 5 + 14 cents) = 98 − 94 cents = 4 cents

Chapter 26

Word Problems in Addition and Subtraction

In the last three chapters your child solved a lot of addition and subtraction problems. In the addition problems he learned about carrying. Then he learned borrowing when he did the subtraction problems.

Now we're going to add words to the numbers. In Minilesson 67, we'll be doing addition word problems, and in Minilesson 68, subtraction word problems. In Minilesson 69, we'll do word problems that call for both addition and subtraction. For all of them, your child will need to use his new carrying and borrowing skills. Let him do Minilessons 67 through 69 on his own, but check his work and be sure to ask him if he needs any help.

MINILESSON 67

Word Problems in Addition

The trick to doing word problems is to form an equation and then solve it.

Let's try the first word problem: Mary drank eight glasses of water today, Juan drank seven glasses, and Oleg drank nine. What was the total number of glasses of water that they drank today?

Answer: 8 glasses + 7 glasses + 9 glasses = 24 glasses

You can also set up the equation this way:

$$\begin{array}{r} 1 \\ 8 \\ 7 \\ \underline{9} \\ 24 \end{array}$$

Now go on to Problem Set A.

Problem Set A

1. Mr. Lundquist bought three shirts. He paid 12 dollars for the first shirt, 14 dollars for the second, and 15 dollars for the third. How much did he pay for the three shirts?

2. Marty Russo scored 22 points in his first basketball game. If he scored 39 points in his second game, what was the total number of points he scored in both games?

3. If Pei has 15 baseball cards, Pedro has 28 baseball cards, and Neil has 37 baseball cards, how many cards do they have altogether?

4. How much is 36 plus 59?

5. How much is 28 plus 48?

6. If Eleni has 22 books, Justine has 29 books, and Sophie has 17 books, how many books do they have altogether?

7. How much is 15 plus 28 plus 39?

8. Agatha has 24 cents. Jane has 17 cents. Steve has 28 cents. How much money do they have altogether?

9. How much is 33 plus 28 plus 17?

10. How much is 9 plus 26 plus 38?

Answers on page 215.

MINILESSON 68

Word Problems in Subtraction

Just as with addition word problems, to do subtraction word problems you need to form an equation and then solve it.

Try this one: Mrs. Poulos owed Mr. Ryan 62 dollars. If she paid him 25 dollars, how much money did she still owe?

Answer:

$$\begin{array}{r} \overset{5}{\cancel{6}}\overset{1}{2} \\ -25 \\ \hline 37 \text{ dollars} \end{array}$$

Let's go over this step by step.

First we set it up as a subtraction problem. $\begin{array}{r} 62 \\ -25 \\ \hline \end{array}$

Then we borrow one 10 from 62. $\begin{array}{r} \overset{5}{\cancel{6}}\overset{1}{2} \\ -25 \\ \hline \end{array}$

And finally, we subtract. $\begin{array}{r} \overset{}{\cancel{6}}\overset{1}{2} \\ -25 \\ \hline 37 \text{ dollars} \end{array}$

Now try Problem Set B.

Problem Set B

1. How much is 31 minus 14?

2. If a store had 81 air conditioners in the morning and sold 44 during the day, how many air conditioners were left at the end of the day?

3. Mr. Ruggiero caught 72 fish. He gave away 49. How many fish did he have left?

4. If you began the day with 94 marbles and lost 36, how many marbles would you have left?

5. If your house has 32 windows and 19 are open, how many windows are not open?

6. Samantha started the day with 25 doughnuts. In the morning she ate three and gave four to Mark. She ate two in the afternoon. After dinner she ate three more. How many doughnuts did she have left?

7. George baked 56 cookies. The cookie monster grabbed 19. How many are left?

8. There were 32 girls and 16 boys at a party. How many more girls than boys were at the party?

9. There were 90 dogs and cats at the animal shelter. If 48 found homes, how many animals were left in the shelter?

10. There are 82 teachers at the Elm Street School. If 49 of the teachers are women, how many of the teachers are men?

Answers on page 216.

MINILESSON 69

Combination Word Problems

In Minilesson 67, you did addition word problems. Then, in Minilesson 68, you did subtraction word problems. Now you're going to do addition and subtraction in the same word problems. To do these combination problems, you still need to form equations and solve them.

Try doing this one: Maria had 32 cents. She gave 14 cents to Joseph. Then Inga gave Maria 45 cents. How much money does Maria have?

Answer:

$$32 - 14 + 45 = ?$$

This can be broken down into two problems.

First we subtract 14 cents from 32 cents:

$$\overset{2\ 1}{\cancel{3}2} \\ \underline{-14} \\ 18 \text{ cents}$$

Then we add 18 cents and 45 cents:

$$\overset{1}{}18 \\ \underline{+45} \\ 63 \text{ cents}$$

Let's do another one: Sonia had 27 marbles. Yolanda gave her 14 more. Then Sonia gave 22 marbles to Steve. How many marbles did Sonia have left?

Answer:

$27 + 14 - 22 = ?$

Again, let's break this down into two problems:

$$\overset{1}{}27 \\ \underline{+14} \\ 41$$

Now we do some subtraction:

$$\overset{3\ 1}{\cancel{4}1} \\ \underline{-22} \\ 19$$

Here's a problem set for you to do.

Problem Set C

1. How much is 15 plus 16 minus 12?

2. Sally had 54 pieces of candy. Luis gave her 17 more. Then Sally gave 23 pieces of candy to Marika. How many pieces of candy did Sally have left?

3. Harry brought 62 crackers to eat with his soup. Joan brought 35 crackers. How many crackers altogether did they bring? How many more crackers did Harry bring than Joan brought?

4. Forty-two children went on a train ride. At the first stop, eight children got off and six got on. How many children are now on the train?

5. Twenty-six children were at the party at one o'clock. By two o'clock four children had left and ten new children had come to the party. How many children were at the party at two o'clock?

6. How much is 56 minus 37 plus 13?

7. You begin the day with 12 cents. Paul gives you 15 cents, and then you give 9 cents to Larry. How much money do you have left?

8. Sixteen people were on a bus when it stopped at Main Street. Four people got off and eleven more got on. How many people are now on the bus?

9. There are 17 boys and 12 girls in a class. How many children altogether are in the class? How many more boys than girls are in the class?

10. How much is 22 plus 48 minus 31?

Answers on page 216.

Answers to Chapter 26 Problem Sets

Problem Set A

	1		1		2		1		1
1.	12	**2.**	22	**3.**	15	**4.**	36	**5.**	28
	14		+39		28		+59		+48
	15		61 points		37		95		76
	41 dollars				80 cards				

	1		2		1		1		2
6.	22	**7.**	15	**8.**	24	**9.**	33	**10.**	9
	29		28		17		28		26
	17		39		28		17		38
	68 books		82		69 cents		78		73

Problem Set B

1. ²¹ $\cancel{3}1$
      -14
        17

2. ⁷¹ $\cancel{8}1$
      -44
        37 air conditioners

3. ⁶¹ $\cancel{7}2$
      -49
        23 fish

4. ⁸¹ $\cancel{9}4$
      -36
        58 marbles

5. ²¹ $\cancel{3}2$
      -19
        13

6. 3
        4
        2
        $\underline{3}$
       12

         25
       -12
        13 doughnuts

7. ⁴¹ $\cancel{5}6$
      -19
        37 cookies

8. ²¹ $\cancel{3}2$
      -16
        16

9. ⁸¹ $\cancel{9}0$
      -48
        42 animals

10. ⁷¹ $\cancel{8}2$
       -49
        33 men

Problem Set C

1. ¹ 15
       $+16$
        31

        ²¹ $\cancel{3}1$
       -12
        19

2. ¹ 54
       $+17$
        71

        ⁶¹ $\cancel{7}1$
       -23
        48 pieces

3. 62
       $+35$
        97 altogether

        ⁵¹ $\cancel{6}2$
       -35
        27 more

4. ³¹ $\cancel{4}2$
       $- 8$
        34

        ¹ 34
       $+ 6$
        40 children

5. 26
       $- 4$
        22

         22
       $+10$
        32 children

6. ⁴¹ $\cancel{5}6$
       -37
        19

        ¹ 19
       $+13$
        32

7. 12
       $+15$
        27

        ¹¹ $\cancel{2}7$
       $- 9$
        18 cents

8. 16
       $- 4$
        12

         12
       $+11$
        23 people

9. 17
       $+12$
        29 altogether

         17
       -12
        5 more

10. ¹ 22
       $+48$
        70

        ⁶¹ $\cancel{7}0$
       -31
        39

Chapter 27

Telling Time

Telling time is obviously an important skill. While different children develop this skill at different times, by the end of second grade your child should be able to tell time on both digital and conventional clocks.

If your child has trouble telling time, sit down with her for a few minutes a day and ask her what time it is on a watch. Then change the time and see if she can tell you what time it is.

Is the skill of telling time essential to learning arithmetic? If your child falls behind her classmates in the ability to tell time, will this prevent her from learning more advanced mathematical skills? The answer to both questions is a definite no. But telling time is still important, and learning how to do it will increase your child's comfort level with numbers.

In Minilesson 70, we'll look at the mechanics of telling time—questions like how many seconds there are in a minute, how many minutes there are in an hour, and how time is read from a clock. In Minilesson 71, we'll tell time with conventional clocks, and in Minilesson 72, we'll tell time with digital clocks.

If your child can read well enough and is somewhat familiar with telling time, have her read through the minilessons on her own. Otherwise, go through them with her. Be sure to check her work either way.

MINILESSON 70

Telling Time in Words and Numbers

In this minilesson we're going to talk about minutes and hours. And the only thing you'll need to remember is that there are 60 minutes in an hour.

Let's say that the time is a quarter after one, or a quarter past one. One quarter of an hour is 15 minutes. If we were to divide a 60-minute hour into four equal parts, each part would be 15 minutes, or a quarter of an hour. We can write a quarter past one as 1:15.

If the time were twenty after four, or 20 minutes past four, we could write it as 4:20.

Now here's a tricky one. How would you write the time ten of eight, or ten to eight? You can write it as 7:50. How do we get 7:50? If there are 60 minutes in an hour, then in 10 minutes it will be eight o'clock. So we can subtract 10 minutes from 60 minutes to get 50 minutes.

$$
\begin{array}{r}
60 \\
-10 \\
\hline
50
\end{array}
$$

In other words, 50 minutes have already gone by since seven o'clock, so the time is 7:50.

How much is sixty past seven? The answer is eight o'clock. So if 60 minutes past seven is eight o'clock, then 50 minutes past seven is 7:50, or ten to eight.

Here's another one: How would you write the time twenty of eleven? There are 60 minutes in an hour, right? If we're 20 minutes short of eleven o'clock, then 40 minutes have passed since ten o'clock. That makes the time 10:40. Here's how it would look as a subtraction problem:

$$
\begin{array}{r}
60 \\
-20 \\
\hline
40
\end{array}
$$

Let's do one more. Write the numbers for the time five of three.

The answer is 2:55. Five of three means that 55 minutes have passed since two o'clock. So we have 2:55. Just remember that an hour has 60 minutes. If it's five of three, just take 60 and subtract $5: 60 - 5 = 55$.

If you're having trouble, ask your parent to go through the minilesson with you. If you understood all of this, try Problem Set A on your own.

Problem Set A

1. Write the time in numbers for each of these times:

a. a quarter of four

d. ten of nine

b. twenty of twelve

e. twenty-five of ten

c. twenty after eight

f. five of four

2. Write the time in words for each of these times:

a. 5:25

d. 11:40

b. 12:50

e. 2:05

c. 3:30

f. 8:45

Answers on page 224.

MINILESSON 71

Telling Time on Conventional Clocks

There are two types of clocks. The older, conventional type is usually round-faced, and has numbers around a circle. The number 12 is always on top and the number 6 is always on the bottom. The second type of clock is the digital clock. It has just three or four numbers in the middle.

Wristwatches can also be divided into these two types. If you own a conventional watch this minilesson will probably be very easy for you.

We're going to work with the conventional clock or watch right now. We'll look at the digital clock in the next minilesson. Now let's see how well you can tell time.

Telling time is easy when you know what each number on the clock face stands for. We read the hour with the smaller, or shorter, hour hand and the minutes with the larger, or longer, minute hand. How would you write the time on each of these two clocks?

The first answer is a quarter after one, or 1:15. What do we mean when we say "a quarter"? We mean a quarter of an hour. And what do we mean when we say "1:15"? We mean 15 minutes after the hour of one. Fifteen minutes is a quarter of an hour, which is 60 minutes.

What time is it on the clock to the right? It's a quarter to five, or 4:45. In other words, we can say that in a quarter of an hour, or in 15 minutes, it will be five o'clock. When we say it's 4:45, we're saying it's 45 minutes past the hour of four.

On these two clock faces, draw hands to show the times written below each.

a quarter after six   a quarter to eleven

Did your clocks look like these?

In the set of problems that follows, you'll be asked to tell time on clock faces and draw hands on blank clock faces.

Problem Set B

Write down the time shown on each clock below.

1. _____ 2. _____ 3. _____ 4. _____

5. _____ 6. _____ 7. _____ 8. _____

On the blank clock faces, draw hands to show the times given below each:

9. twenty after nine **10.** twenty-five of eight **11.** ten before six **12.** twenty-five after seven

13. a quarter of ten

14. a quarter after twelve

15. ten after eleven

16. five after two

Answers on pages 224–225.

MINILESSON 72

Telling Time on Digital Clocks

In Minilesson 70 we went over changing words into numbers and numbers into words. In Minilesson 71 we covered telling time using conventional clocks and watches. Now we're going to use digital clocks and watches to tell time.

First try to figure out how you would say the time on these two digital clocks:

The answer to the first one is five after four, or four-oh-five. The answer to the second is ten of two, or ten to two, or one fifty.

Now let's try something that's a little harder. If it's a quarter of three, how would that time look on a digital clock or watch? It would read: 2:45.

If it's a quarter after one, how would that time look on a digital watch? Write your answer in the box.

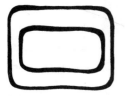

Your answer should look like this:

How would the time five of four look on a digital clock? Write your answer in this box:

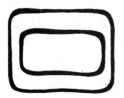

The answer would look like this:

Now try this set of problems.

Problem Set C

1. *Write how you would say the time on each of these watches or clocks:*

a. _____   b. _____   c. _____

d. _____   e. _____   f. _____

2. *Show how each time given would appear on a digital clock or watch:*

a. ten after five　　**b.** a quarter to eight　　**c.** twenty-five of twelve

d. ten of one　　　**e.** a quarter after eleven　　**f.** five of eight

Answers on page 225.

Answers to Chapter 27 Problem Sets

Problem Set A

1. **a.** 3:45　　　　**d.** 8:50
   b. 11:40　　　**e.** 9:35
   c. 8:20　　　　**f.** 3:55

2. **a.** twenty-five after five, or five twenty-five
   b. ten of one, or twelve fifty
   c. three thirty, or half past three
   d. twenty of twelve, or eleven forty
   e. five after two
   f. eight forty-five, or a quarter to nine

Problem Set B.

1. twenty of two, or one forty
2. ten of three, or two fifty
3. twenty after six, or six twenty
4. twenty-five of one, or twelve thirty-five
5. five of four, or three fifty-five
6. twenty-five after two, or two twenty-five
7. ten after three, or three ten
8. a quarter of five, or four forty-five

9.   10.   11.   12.

13.   14.   15.   16.

Problem Set C

1. **a.** a quarter after six, or six fifteen
    b. seven fifty-five, or five of eight
    c. twelve forty, or twenty of one
    d. three thirty-five, or twenty-five of four
    e. nine forty-five, or a quarter of ten
    f. two fifty, or ten of three

2. **a.** 5:10   **b.** 7:45   **c.** 11:35

    d. 12:50   **e.** 11:15   **f.** 7:55

Chapter 28

Advanced Counting

In this chapter, your child will be counting not only from 1 to 1,000 but up to 50 or 100 by 2s, 3s, 4s, 5s, and 10s. Your child's competence in counting is essential to learning not just addition and subtraction but also multiplication and division. These two concepts will be introduced in the next chapter. Let your child do this chapter on his own, but check his work after he completes each minilesson.

MINILESSON 73

Counting from 1 to 1,000

By the end of the second grade you should be able to count up to 1,000. And you should also be able to write the words that go with the numbers from 1 (one) to 100 (one hundred).

Can you count to 1,000? I am sure that by this time you can definitely count to 100. You don't have to count from 100 to 1,000 right now, but do look over these numbers and make sure that you know all the numbers that come between them:

100, 101, 102, 103,...197, 198, 199, 200, 201, 202, 203,...298, 299, 300, 301, 302,...398, 399, 400, 401, 402,...498, 499, 500, 501, 502,...598, 599, 600, 601, 602,...698, 699, 700, 701, 702,...798, 799, 800, 801, 802,...898, 899, 900, 901, 902,...998, 999, 1,000.

If you feel confident that you know these numbers, then go on to Problem Set A. If you don't, please ask your parent to go over these numbers with you.

Problem Set A

In the space below, write the numbers from 51 to 100. And next to each number, write the word. I'll start you off:

51 <u>fifty-one</u>   68 _____   _____

52 <u>fifty-two</u>   _____   _____

53 _____   _____   _____

54 _____   _____   _____

_____   _____   _____

_____   _____   _____

_____   _____   _____

_____   _____   _____

_____   _____   _____

_____   _____   _____

_____   _____   _____

_____   _____   _____

_____   _____   _____

_____   _____   _____

Answers on page 232.

███ **MINILESSON 74** ███

Filling in the Missing Numbers

Can you fill in the missing numbers? See if you can fill in the blanks in this line of numbers:

278, 279, _____, 281, _____, 283, _____, _____

Here are the missing numbers: 280, 282, 284, 285.

   If you got these right, then you're ready to do Problem Set B. If you didn't, have your parent help you before you do this problem set.

Problem Set B

Fill in the blanks in each line of numbers:

1. 596, _____, 598, _____, _____, 601, _____, _____

2. 992, _____, 994, _____, _____, 997, _____, _____, _____

3. _____, 500, _____, 502, _____, _____, 505, _____, 507, _____

4. 266, _____, 268, _____, _____, 271, _____, 273, _____

5. _____, _____, _____, 801, 802, _____, _____, 805, _____, _____

6. 434, _____, _____, 437, _____, 439, _____, _____, _____

7. 623, _____, _____, 626, _____, 628, _____, _____, _____

8. _____, _____, 397, _____, _____, _____, 401, 402, _____, _____

Answers on page 232.

MINILESSON 75

Counting by 2s, 3s, 4s, 5s, and 10s

In this minilesson, you're going to be counting not only by 2s, but also by 3s, 4s, 5s, and 10s. The reason I'm asking you to do all this is that the next minilesson will introduce you to multiplication, which can actually be done by counting by 2s, 3s, 4s, 5s, 10s, and a few other numbers.

Very briefly, when you're counting by 2s, starting with 2, you count like this:

$$2, 4, 6, 8, 10, \ldots$$

Counting by 3s:

$$3, 6, 9, 12, 15, \ldots$$

And counting by 5s:

$$5, 10, 15, 20, 25, \ldots$$

So let's get started.

Problem Set C

1. Count by 2s from 2 to 50.

2. Count by 3s from 3 to 48.

3. Count by 4s from 4 to 48.

4. Count by 5s from 5 to 100.

5. Count by 10s from 10 to 100.

Answers on page 232.

How did you do? If you got everything right, then go directly to chapter 29. If you didn't, please read the Extra Help box.

Counting by 2s, 3s, 4s, 5s, and 10s

Counting by 2s is exactly like counting by 1s, except we only count every *other* number. So instead of counting by 1s—1, 2, 3, 4, 5, 6, 7, 8, 9, 10—we start with 2 and count every other number—2, 4, 6, 8, 10.

To see how this is done, write all the numbers from 1 to 50, without skipping any. Once you've done that, cross out every other number, starting with 1, 3, 5.

Here's what you should have:

1̶ 2 3̶ 4 5̶ 6 7̶ 8 9̶ 10 1̶1̶ 12 1̶3̶ 14 1̶5̶ 16 1̶7̶ 18 1̶9̶
20 2̶1̶ 22 2̶3̶ 24 2̶5̶ 26 2̶7̶ 28 2̶9̶ 30 3̶1̶ 32 3̶3̶ 34 3̶5̶
36 3̶7̶ 38 3̶9̶ 40 4̶1̶ 42 4̶3̶ 44 4̶5̶ 46 4̶7̶ 48 4̶9̶ 50

Now read what you have left.

What you've just done is counted by 2s from 2 to 50. Now try counting out loud by 2s without looking at the numbers. Ask your parent to listen to you count to make sure that you're counting correctly.

Next we'll try counting by 3s. Write all the numbers from 1 to 50 without skipping any numbers. Now cross off 1 and 2, leave 3, cross off 4 and 5, leave 6, and keep crossing off two numbers and leaving one. I'll start you off: 1̶ 2̶ 3 4̶ 5̶ 6 7̶ 8̶ 9. Keep crossing off two numbers and leaving one all the way through 50.

What you did should look like this:

1̶ 2̶ 3 4̶ 5̶ 6 7̶ 8̶ 9 1̶0̶ 1̶1̶ 12 1̶3̶ 1̶4̶ 15 1̶6̶ 1̶7̶ 18 1̶9̶
2̶0̶ 21 2̶2̶ 2̶3̶ 24 2̶5̶ 2̶6̶ 27 2̶8̶ 2̶9̶ 30 3̶1̶ 3̶2̶ 33 3̶4̶ 3̶5̶
36 3̶7̶ 3̶8̶ 39 4̶0̶ 4̶1̶ 42 4̶3̶ 4̶4̶ 45 4̶6̶ 4̶7̶ 48 4̶9̶ 5̶0̶

Now read the numbers you have left.

You've just counted by 3s from 3 to 48. Now try counting out loud by 3s without looking at the numbers. Ask your parent to listen to you count to make sure that you're doing it right.

Now we'll count by 4s. Again, write all the numbers from 1 to 50. Then cross off the first three numbers—1, 2, and 3—leave the fourth number, 4, cross out the next three—5, 6, and 7—leave 8, and cross out the next three. So what you need to do is cross off three numbers, leave one, cross off another three numbers, and leave one, until you've gotten to 50.

Have you done all of that? Then what you did was this:

~~1~~ ~~2~~ ~~3~~ 4 ~~5~~ ~~6~~ ~~7~~ 8 ~~9~~ ~~10~~ ~~11~~ 12 ~~13~~ ~~14~~ ~~15~~ 16 ~~17~~ ~~18~~ ~~19~~
20 ~~21~~ ~~22~~ ~~23~~ 24 ~~25~~ ~~26~~ ~~27~~ 28 ~~29~~ ~~30~~ ~~31~~ 32 ~~33~~ ~~34~~ ~~35~~
36 ~~37~~ ~~38~~ ~~39~~ 40 ~~41~~ ~~42~~ ~~43~~ 44 ~~45~~ ~~46~~ ~~47~~ 48 ~~49~~ ~~50~~

Read these numbers—4, 8, 12, 16, …all the way up to 48. Then see if you can recite them without looking.

Next comes counting by 5s. See if you can write the numbers from 5 to 100 yourself, counting by 5s. This one is actually easier than counting by 3s or 4s because every number will end in either 5 or 0.

Did you get this?

5, 10, 15, 20, 25, 30, 35, 40, 45, 50, 55, 60, 65, 70, 75, 80, 85, 90, 95, 100

If you didn't get any of these right, please ask your parent to help you.

Your child needs to be able to count by 2s, 3s, 4s, 5s, and 10s by the end of second grade. If you find that your child is having difficulty doing some of this, please go back over this entire mini-lesson with her. If necessary, make up flash cards. If your child can count to 100, then she can easily learn to count by 2s, 3s, 4s, 5s, and 10s.

Answers to Chapter 28 Problem Sets

Problem Set A

51	fifty-one	68	sixty-eight	85	eighty-five
52	fifty-two	69	sixty-nine	86	eighty-six
53	fifty-three	70	seventy	87	eighty-seven
54	fifty-four	71	seventy-one	88	eighty-eight
55	fifty-five	72	seventy-two	89	eighty-nine
56	fifty-six	73	seventy-three	90	ninety
57	fifty-seven	74	seventy-four	91	ninety-one
58	fifty-eight	75	seventy-five	92	ninety-two
59	fifty-nine	76	seventy-six	93	ninety-three
60	sixty	77	seventy-seven	94	ninety-four
61	sixty-one	78	seventy-eight	95	ninety-five
62	sixty-two	79	seventy-nine	96	ninety-six
63	sixty-three	80	eighty	97	ninety-seven
64	sixty-four	81	eighty-one	98	ninety-eight
65	sixty-five	82	eighty-two	99	ninety-nine
66	sixty-six	83	eighty-three	100	one hundred
67	sixty-seven	84	eighty-four		

Problem Set B

1. 597, 599, 600, 602, 603
2. 993, 995, 996, 998, 999, 1,000
3. 499, 501, 503, 504, 506, 508
4. 267, 269, 270, 272, 274
5. 798, 799, 800, 803, 804, 806, 807
6. 435, 436, 438, 440, 441, 442
7. 624, 625, 627, 629, 630, 631
8. 395, 396, 398, 399, 400, 403, 404

Problem Set C

1. 2, 4, 6, 8, 10, 12, 14, 16, 18, 20, 22, 24, 26, 28, 30, 32, 34, 36, 38, 40, 42, 44, 46, 48, 50
2. 3, 6, 9, 12, 15, 18, 21, 24, 27, 30, 33, 36, 39, 42, 45, 48
3. 4, 8, 12, 16, 20, 24, 28, 32, 36, 40, 44, 48
4. 5, 10, 15, 20, 25, 30, 35, 40, 45, 50, 55, 60, 65, 70, 75, 80, 85, 90, 95, 100
5. 10, 20, 30, 40, 50, 60, 70, 80, 90, 100

Introduction to Multiplication and Division

In many schools, multiplication and division are introduced as early as the second grade. The idea is to expose children to these mathematical tools, so that when they are applied more rigorously in the third and fourth grades, the children will already be familiar with them. In Minilesson 76, your child will be doing several simple multiplication problems, and in Minilesson 77, she will be introduced to division but will not be expected to solve any problems until she reaches the third grade. Let your child do Minilessons 76 and 77 on her own, but stand by to answer any questions. After she completes them, check her answers for Problem Set A.

MINILESSON 76

Introduction to Multiplication

Multiplication is really fast addition. For example, how much is 3 times 4? It can be figured out like this:

$$4 + 4 + 4 = 12$$

In the previous minilesson we were counting by 2s, 3s, 4s, 5s, and 10s. This was a step toward multiplication. Now we're going to take another step.

Below we have two rows of circles. There are four circles in each row. How many circles are there altogether?

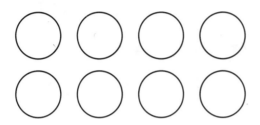

4 × 2 = 8
This is read:
4 times 2 equals 8.

There are eight circles. There are four ways to find that answer. The first way is to count every circle. The second way is to add: 4 + 4 = 8. The third way is also to add: 2 + 2 + 2 + 2 = 8. And the fourth way is to multiply the four circles times the two rows. We write that problem like this: 4 × 2 = 8. Any way you do it, you get eight circles.

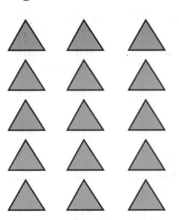

Here's another question for you. How many triangles do you see here?

3 × 5 = 15

Did you get 15 triangles? How did you get your answer? One way would have been to count all the triangles. A second way would have been to add: 3 + 3 + 3 + 3 + 3 = 15. Or, you could have added down instead of across: 5 + 5 + 5 = 15. But a faster way of doing this problem is multiplication: 3 triangles × 5 rows = 15 triangles.

In order to do multiplication, you need to memorize a whole table of numbers. But you don't have to learn that table until the third grade. Right now we're just getting in some practice, so when you're in the third grade, you'll already know how to do some multiplication.

Now try to figure out how much is 4 times 4, which we write as 4 × 4. First draw four rows of circles, with four circles in each row in the space below.

How many circles do you have? You should have 16. Again, you can find the answer by counting all the circles, or by adding: 4 + 4 + 4 + 4 = 16. Or by multiplying: 4 × 4 = 16. Any way you do it, the answer will be 16.

$$4 \times 4 = 16$$

Now draw six rows of squares, with five squares in each row.

How many squares do you have? There are 30. You can get this answer by counting up all the squares, or by adding: 5 + 5 + 5 + 5 + 5 + 5 = 30.

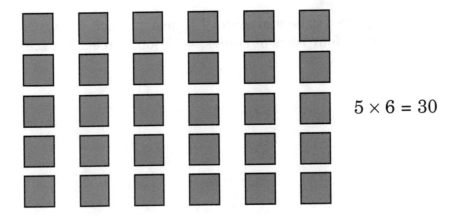

$5 \times 6 = 30$

Multiplication is a shortcut to addition. You will be doing plenty of multiplication problems in the third grade. But I think you're ready to do some shorter ones, like those in Problem Set A. Give it a try. If it helps, you can draw rows of circles, triangles, or squares for each problem on a separate sheet of paper.

Problem Set A

1. How much is 2 times 7?

2. How much is 5 times 4?

3. How much is 3 times 2?

4. How much is 4 times 4?

5. How much is 10×3?

6. How much is 6×2?

7. How much is 5×5?

8. How much is 4×10?

Answers on page 238.

MINILESSON 77

Introduction to Division

Division is the opposite of multiplication, just as subtraction is the opposite of addition. In the last minilesson we had this multiplication problem: How much is 3 times 5? We drew five rows of triangles, with three triangles in each row →

Then we added the rows: 3 + 3 + 3 + 3 + 3 = 15. Now we'll see why division is the opposite of multiplication.

How much is 15 divided by 3? To answer this question, we divide the triangles into three equal groups →

So how much is 15 divided by 3? The answer is 5. The number 15 is really three rows of five. So 15 divided by 3 is 5. This is written 15 ÷ 3 = 5.

Next question: How much is 15 divided by 5? We divide the triangles into five equal groups →

How many triangles are in each part? The answer is 3. So 15 ÷ 5 = 3.

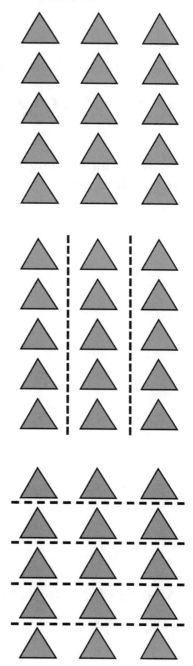

Ready for another one? How much is 10 divided by 2? Just draw 10 X's in a row in the space below, and then divide the line in half.

Did your answer come out to 5? Here's all you had to do:

$$10 \div 2 = 5$$

Well, that's enough division for now. You'll get to do a lot more in the third grade.

Answers for Chapter 29

Problem Set A

1. 14	**2.** 20	**3.** 6	**4.** 16
5. 30	**6.** 12	**7.** 25	**8.** 40

Chapter 30

Shapes and Measurements

In this chapter we'll talk about geometric shapes, fractions, and measurements in inches, feet, and yards. Your child will need a ruler and, if you happen to have one, a yardstick or a tape measure.

Fractions, which were introduced in Minilessons 36 and 37 in first-grade math, are reintroduced in Minilesson 78. It would be a good idea to review these earlier minilessons with your child before he begins Minilesson 78. Minilesson 79 introduces measurements in inches, feet, and yards. Because these minilessons are a little harder than the ones we've been doing, go over them with your child.

By the end of the second grade your child should be familiar with fractions ranging from $\frac{1}{2}$, $\frac{1}{3}$, $\frac{1}{4}$, and $\frac{1}{5}$ to $\frac{1}{6}$, $\frac{1}{8}$, $\frac{1}{10}$, and $\frac{1}{100}$.

This is the last chapter of the book. After the chapter, there's a final exam for your child to take.

MINILESSON 78

Fractions

It shouldn't take more than a few minutes to go over this minilesson with your child. A good way of introducing fractions is by shading parts of circles, squares, rectangles, and other geometric figures. The following chart shows a few examples.

Ask your child to figure out what fraction of each geometric figure is shaded. Have him write his answers below the figures.

1/6 30   1/2   1/4

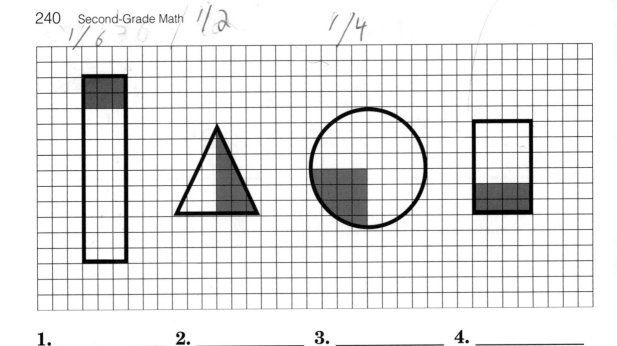

1. _____ 2. _____ 3. _____ 4. _____

Answers:
1. one-sixth (⅙) **2.** one-half (½) **3.** one-fourth (¼) **4.** one-third (⅓)

Another useful tool in learning about fractions is a ruler. This ruler is magnified four times (so it is four times bigger than an actual ruler). Find on it the half-inch marker and the quarter-inch markers, then draw a short line next to each.

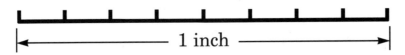

|← —————— 1 inch —————— →|

Answer:

$\frac{1}{4}$ $\frac{1}{2}$ $\frac{3}{4}$ $\frac{4}{4}$

$(\frac{2}{4})$ (1)

Can you mark off the eighth-inch markers?

Answer:

$\frac{1}{8}$ $\frac{2}{8}$ $\frac{3}{8}$ $\frac{4}{8}$ $\frac{5}{8}$ $\frac{6}{8}$ $\frac{7}{8}$ $\frac{8}{8}$

($\frac{1}{2}$)   (1)

MINILESSON 79

Yards, Feet, and Inches

Have your child work through this minilesson, but sit with her so you can help her.

How many inches are there in a foot? The answer is 12. And how many feet are there in a yard? The answer is 3.

Once you know that there are 12 inches in a foot, and that there are 3 feet in a yard, you're ready to answer the following questions.

Feet and Inches

There are 12 inches in 1 foot. How many inches are there in 2 feet? We set this up as an equation: 12 + 12 = 24. So there are 24 inches in 2 feet.

Fill in the blank:

1 foot 6 inches = _____ inches

To find the answer, you set up the equation this way:

12 inches + 6 inches = 18 inches

Now let's change inches into feet. We already know that there are 12 inches in 1 foot. How would you do this problem?

32 inches = _____ feet _____ inches

Solution:

32 inches = 12 inches (1 foot) + 12 inches (1 foot) + 8 inches
32 inches = 2 feet 8 inches

Here's a problem set on feet and inches.

Problem Set A

Set up an equation for each, and fill in the blanks with the answers.

1. 2 feet 4 inches = _____ inches

2. 1 foot 9 inches = _____ inches

3. 3 feet = _____ inches

4. 24 inches = _____ feet

5. 20 inches = _____ foot _____ inches

6. 26 inches = _____ feet _____ inches

Answers on page 244.

Yards, Feet, and Inches

There are 3 feet in a yard and 12 inches in a foot. So how many inches are there in a yard? Each of the 3 feet has 12 inches, so to get your answer, 36, you need to add: Remember how to add three numbers together?

$$12$$
$$12$$
$$\underline{12}$$
$$36$$

Fill in the blank:

$$6 \text{ feet} = \text{\_\_\_ yards}$$

The answer is 2 yards. How did we do this? If 3 feet equals 1 yard, then 6 feet equals 2 yards, because 3 + 3 = 6.

There are _____ inches in 1 yard 1 foot.

The answer is 48 inches. This problem can be done in two parts. First we change everything into feet. One yard equals 3 feet. Since we began with 1 yard 1 foot, we have 3 feet + 1 foot = 4 feet. Then we change feet into inches. One foot equals 12 inches. How many inches are there in 4 feet? We find the answer, 48, by adding:

$$
\begin{array}{r}
12 \\
12 \\
12 \\
\underline{12} \\
48
\end{array}
$$

Two more problem sets and then, believe it or not, we have covered all you need to know in second-grade math.

Problem Set B

Set up equations and then fill in the blanks.

1. 36 inches = _____ feet

2. 36 inches = _____ yard

3. 40 inches = _____ feet _____ inches

4. 40 inches = _____ yard _____ inches

5. 2 yards = _____ inches

6. 2 yards = _____ feet

Answers on page 244.

Problem Set C

Fill in the blanks:

1. 2 feet = _____ inches

2. 1 yard 1 foot = _____ inches

3. 2 feet 3 inches = _____ inches

4. 1 yard 5 inches = _____ inches

5. 1 foot 9 inches = _____ inches

6. 2 yards = _____ inches

7. 1 yard 2 feet = _____ inches

8. 1 yard 1 foot 10 inches = _____ inches

Answers on page 245.

Answers to Chapter 30 Problem Sets

Problem Set A
1. 2 feet 4 inches = 12 + 12 + 4 inches = 28 inches
2. 1 foot 9 inches = 12 + 9 inches = 21 inches
3. 3 feet = 12 + 12 + 12 inches = 36 inches
4. 24 inches = 12 + 12 inches = 2 feet
5. 20 inches = 12 + 8 inches = 1 foot 8 inches
6. 26 inches = 12 + 12 + 2 inches = 2 feet 2 inches

Problem Set B
1. 36 inches = 12 + 12 + 12 inches = 3 feet
2. 36 inches = 12 + 12 + 12 inches = 1 yard
3. 40 inches = 12 + 12 + 12 + 4 inches = 3 feet 4 inches
4. 40 inches = 36 + 4 inches = 1 yard 4 inches
5. 2 yards = 36 + 36 inches = 72 inches
6. 2 yards = 72 inches = 12 + 12 + 12 + 12 + 12 + 12 inches = 6 feet

Problem Set C
1. 2 feet = 12 + 12 inches = 24 inches
2. 1 yard 1 foot = 36 + 12 inches = 48 inches
3. 2 feet 3 inches = 12 + 12 + 3 inches = 27 inches
4. 1 yard 5 inches = 36 + 5 inches= 41 inches
5. 1 foot 9 inches = 12 + 9 inches = 21 inches
6. 2 yards = 36 + 36 inches = 72 inches
7. 1 yard 2 feet = 36 + 12 + 12 inches = 60 inches
8. 1 yard 1 foot 10 inches = 36 + 12 + 10 inches = 58 inches

Second-Grade Final Exam

Your child has just completed all the math that's taught in the second grade. This exam covers all the material in Chapters 16 through 30—a whole year's work.

This exam is a good chance to appraise your child's progress. Remember that the skills learned in the first two grades are the building blocks for later math success. So it's crucial that he understand and have these skills down cold.

Let's do this exam just like we did the final exam after the first grade, with two rules: 1. no pocket calculators; and 2. it's not an open-book exam.

Since this exam covers an entire year of math, there is no way your child can complete it at one sitting—or even three or four sittings. I would suggest that the entire exam be taken over five or six sittings.

After your child has completed the exam and you have had a chance to check his answers, it will be necessary to go over any concepts that have given him trouble. There are sets of problems from nearly each minilesson. The reason the minilesson numbers are listed is that if your child gets more than one answer wrong in any minilesson, you will need to review that minilesson with him. This will ensure that when he has completed this book, he will know all he needs to know about first- and second-grade math.

Answers on pages 262–268.

Chapter 16. Counting and Writing Numbers up to 200

(Minilessons 40 and 41)

1. *Write the numbers from 190 to 200.*

190, _____, _____, _____, _____, _____, _____,

_____, _____, _____, _____

2. *Write the numbers from 40 to 50, then next to each number write the word.*

40   <u>forty</u>_____   _____

_____   _____

_____   _____

_____   _____

_____   _____

_____

Chapter 17. Mathematical Symbols
(Minilessons 42 through 44)

Problem Set A

Use > or < to complete each statement.

1. 4 ☐ 7

2. 8 ☐ 0

3. 2 ☐ 6

4. 5 ☐ 4

Problem Set B

Use > or < to complete each statement.

1. 4 ☐ 5 + 3

2. 9 ☐ 6 + 2

3. 5 ☐ 9 − 3

4. 3 ☐ 7 − 3

Problem Set C

Use = or ≠ to complete each statement.

1. 7 + 4 ☐ 12 − 1

2. 2 + 12 ☐ 7 + 6

3. 6 − 1 ☐ 9 − 5

4. 3 + 13 ☐ 17 − 1

Problem Set D

Use >, <, or = to complete each statement.

1. 10 + 4 ☐ 18 − 4

2. 2 + 7 ☐ 15 − 7

3. 1 + 7 ☐ 3 + 6

4. 15 − 4 ☐ 6 + 4

5. 19 − 10 ☐ 5 + 5

6. 4 + 13 ☐ 19 − 3

Chapter 18. Grouping Numbers in 10s and 1s
(Minilessons 45 through 47)

1. In the number 35 there are _____ 10s and _____ 1s.

2. In the number 76 there are _____ 10s and _____ 1s.

3. In the number 98 there are _____ 10s and _____ 1s.

4. In the number 31 there are _____ 10s and _____ 1.

5. In the number 46 there are _____ 10s and _____ 1s.

6. What is the number that has seven 10s and four 1s?

7. What is the number that has five 10s and five 1s?

8. What is the number that has eight 10s and seven 1s?

9. What is the number that has one 10 and seven 1s?

10. What is the number that has four 10s and two 1s?

Chapter 19. Adding Three Numbers and Double- and Triple-Digit Numbers
(Minilessons 48 through 50)

Adding Three Numbers (Minilesson 48)

1. 4	2. 3	3. 9	4. 4	5. 3	6. 6
+7	+5	+6	+8	+0	+7
+8	+4	+0	+7	+9	+1

7. 8	8. 6	9. 7	10. 5	11. 4	12. 7
+0	+9	+3	+6	+6	+9
+8	+2	+7	+8	+5	+3

Adding Double- and Triple-Digit Numbers (Minilessons 49 and 50)

1. 43	**2.** 51	**3.** 39	**4.** 72	**5.** 21	**6.** 14
+26	+27	+30	+24	+63	+13
7. 50	**8.** 24	**9.** 33	**10.** 57	**11.** 72	**12.** 84
+37	+14	+46	+10	+16	+15
13. 148	**14.** 491	**15.** 364	**16.** 175	**17.** 362	**18.** 109
+111	+507	+525	+400	+624	+680
19. 226	**20.** 834	**21.** 617	**22.** 415	**23.** 362	**24.** 711
+773	+142	+241	+384	+523	+265

Chapter 20. Subtracting Single-, Double-, and Triple-Digit Numbers
(Minilessons 51 through 53)

Subtracting Single-Digit Numbers (Minilesson 51)

1. 10	**2.** 14	**3.** 17	**4.** 12	**5.** 11	**6.** 10
− 2	− 9	− 10	− 8	− 1	− 7
7. 14	**8.** 13	**9.** 16	**10.** 17	**11.** 12	**12.** 10
− 3	− 8	− 5	− 8	− 5	− 0
13. 13	**14.** 11	**15.** 17	**16.** 15	**17.** 11	**18.** 16
− 2	− 4	− 3	− 8	− 8	− 7

Subtracting Double-Digit Numbers (Minilesson 52)

1. 53 −21	2. 96 −36	3. 41 −20	4. 37 −22	5. 66 −45	6. 35 −23
7. 27 −11	8. 49 −32	9. 98 −81	10. 77 −53	11. 32 −21	12. 56 −36

Subtracting Triple-Digit Numbers (Minilesson 53)

1. 396 −182	2. 864 −231	3. 485 −273	4. 529 −420	5. 822 −602
6. 958 −741	7. 653 −412	8. 783 −142	9. 988 −241	

Chapter 21. Word Problems in Addition and Subtraction
(Minilessons 54 and 55)

1. José had nine pennies. He found six more. How many pennies does José now have?

2. How much is 3 plus 4 plus 5?

3. Marcia has four brown books, seven red books, and three blue books. How many books does Marcia have?

4. Mr. Smith had 8 dollars, Mr. Brown had 5 dollars, and Mrs. Gray had 6 dollars. How much money did the three of them have?

5. Doreen had 18 pennies. She gave five to Stan and seven to Mary. How many pennies does she have left?

6. Mark had 68 marbles. He gave 31 to Juris. How many marbles does he have left?

7. How much is 97 minus 24?

8. Start with the number 19. Subtract 5 from it. Then subtract 4. How much do you have left?

Chapter 22. Regrouping, Expanded Notation, and Graphing
(Minilessons 56 and 57)

Regrouping and Expanded Notation (Minilesson 56)

Regroup and then add these sets of numbers.

1. 24
   +38

2. 53
   +29

3. 49
   +34

4. 67
   +18

Graphing 100s, 10s, and 1s (Minilesson 57)

5. Regroup the number 538. Then use blank graph paper to put the 100s, 10s, and 1s in boxes.

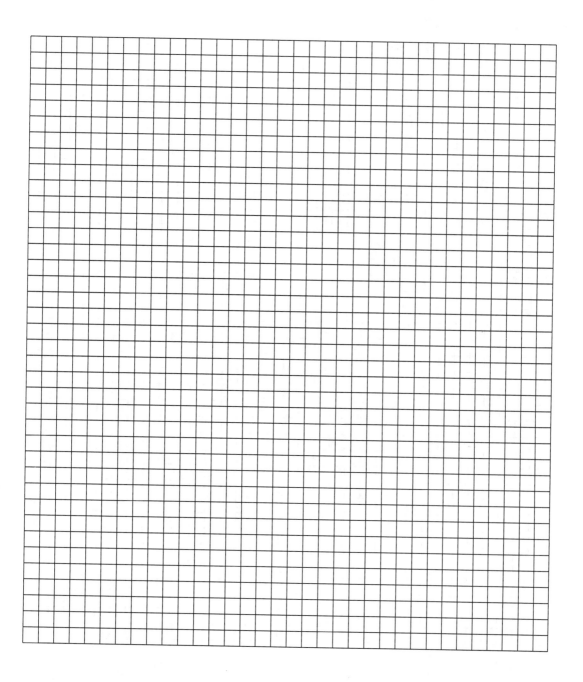

6.   Regroup the number 429. Then use blank graph paper to put the 100s, 10s, and 1s in boxes.

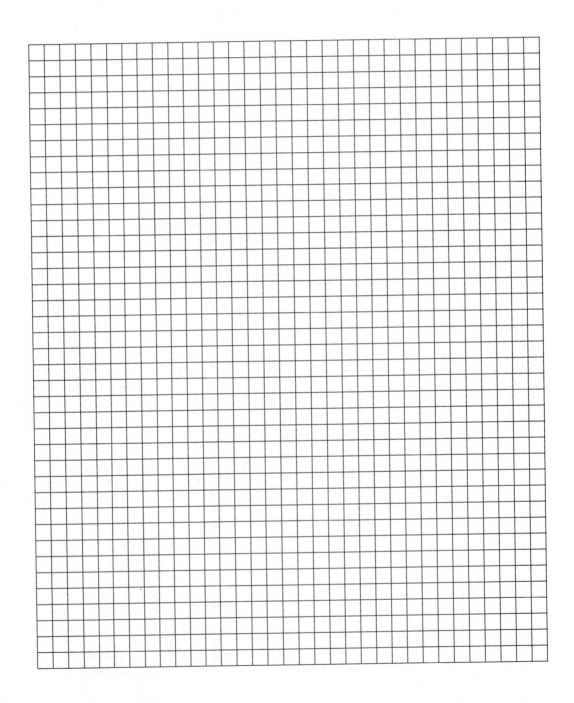

Chapter 23. Addition with Carrying
(Minilessons 59 through 62;
no questions for Minilessons 58 and 60)

Adding Two Double-Digit Numbers with Carrying (Minilesson 59)

1.	22 +49	2.	16 +37	3.	49 +38	4.	26 +49	5.	19 +79	6.	38 +45
7.	77 +14	8.	46 +26	9.	16 +16	10.	24 +46	11.	76 +18	12.	39 +29
13.	55 +38	14.	35 +29	15.	68 +27	16.	72 +19	17.	49 +13	18.	58 +26

Adding Three Double-Digit Numbers with Carrying (Minilesson 61)

1.	21 17 14	2.	36 14 25	3.	10 16 65	4.	15 38 25	5.	29 29 16	6.	38 15 44
7.	20 13 49	8.	53 12 18	9.	28 19 14	10.	47 29 11	11.	57 14 10	12.	63 16 12

Chapter 24. Subtraction with Borrowing and Review of Carrying and Borrowing

(Minilesson 63; no questions for Minilesson 64)

| 1. | 58 −19 | 2. | 61 −37 | 3. | 46 −18 | 4. | 33 −9 | 5. | 80 −22 | 6. | 92 −17 |

| 7. | 34 −18 | 8. | 72 −53 | 9. | 44 −15 | 10. | 64 −39 | 11. | 90 −38 | 12. | 74 −26 |

Chapter 25. Adding and Subtracting Money

(Minilessons 65 and 66)

1. How much is 80 cents minus a dime and a nickel?

2. If you start with 75 cents and spend a quarter, two nickels, and three pennies, how much will you have left?

3. How much is 94 cents minus a quarter, a dime, and four pennies?

4. If you started with 87 cents and spent a quarter, two dimes, and two nickels, how much money would you have left?

5. How much is 92 cents minus two quarters, three nickels, and six pennies?

Chapter 26. Word Problems in Addition and Subtraction

(Minilessons 67 through 69)

1. Sam baked 29 cookies. He ate 5 of them, and Sally ate 7 of them. How many more cookies did Sally eat than Sam ate? How many cookies were left?

2. Fifty-four dogs lived in a kennel. Then six moved out and four moved in. How many dogs were now living in the kennel?

3. There were 10 girls and 7 boys at a party. How many children were at the party? How many more girls than boys were at the party?

4. A man bought five blue books, four black books, and seven red books at a bookstore. How many books did he buy altogether?

5. Mr. Cox bought 80 toys for the children on his block. He gave away 61. How many toys did he have left?

6. There are 94 children in the second grade at the Middletown Elementary School. If 55 of the children are girls, how many are boys?

Chapter 27. Telling Time

(Minilessons 71 and 72; no questions for Minilesson 70)

Telling Time on Conventional Clocks (Minilesson 71)

1. What time is it on these clocks?

a. _____   **b.** _____   **c.** _____   **d.** _____

2. Draw the times indicated on the clock faces below.

a. a quarter after ten   **b.** twenty of six   **c.** twenty-five after nine   **d.** five of four

Telling Time on Digital Clocks (Minilesson 72)

3. What time is it on these clocks?

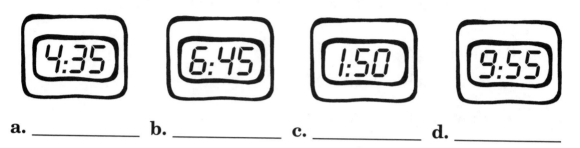

a. _____ **b.** _____ **c.** _____ **d.** _____

4. Please show how these times would appear on each of these clocks:

a. ten after three **b.** five of two **c.** twenty of one **d.** ten of six

Chapter 28. Advanced Counting
(Minilessons 73 through 75)

Write the following numbers in words:

1. 26 _____   **3.** 50 _____

2. 87 _____   **4.** 36 _____

Fill in the missing numbers:

5. 5, 10, _____, 20, _____, 30, 35, _____, 45, _____

6. 198, 199, _____, 201, _____, 203, _____

7. 40, 45, _____, 55, _____, 65, 70, _____, 80, _____

8. 864, 865, _____, 867, _____, 869, 870, _____ 872, _____

Chapter 29. Introduction to Multiplication and Division

(Minilesson 76; no questions for Minilesson 77)

Problem Set A

1. How much is 3 times 8?

2. How much is 5 times 6?

3. How much is 10×7?

4. How much is 2×9?

5. How much is 4×8?

6. How much is 5×9?

Problem Set B

1. How much is 4 times 7?

2. How much is 3 times 9?

3. How much is 4 times 7?

4. How much is 3 times 9?

5. How much is 4×4?

6. How much is 5×6?

7. How much is 10×6?

8. How much is 8×5?

Chapter 30. Shapes and Measurements
(Minilesson 79; no questions for Minilesson 78)

1. How many inches are there in

   a. a foot?

   b. a yard?

2. 24 inches = _____ feet

3. 42 inches = _____ feet _____ inches

4. 2 yards = _____ inches

5. 3 yards = _____ feet

6. 15 feet = _____ yards

7. 30 inches = _____ feet _____ inches

8. 1 foot 4 inches = _____ inches

9. 1 yard 3 inches = _____ inches

Second-Grade Final Exam Answers

Chapter 16. Counting and Writing Numbers up to 200

1. 190, 191, 192, 193, 194, 195, 196, 197, 198, 199, 200

2.
40 forty	46 forty-six
41 forty-one	47 forty-seven
42 forty-two	48 forty-eight
43 forty-three	49 forty-nine
44 forty-four	50 fifty
45 forty-five	

Chapter 17. Mathematical Symbols

Problem Set A
1. $4 < 7$ **2.** $8 > 0$ **3.** $2 < 6$ **4.** $5 > 4$

Problem Set B
1. $4 < 8$ **2.** $9 > 8$ **3.** $5 < 6$ **4.** $3 < 4$

Problem Set C
1. $11 = 11$ **2.** $14 \neq 13$ **3.** $5 \neq 4$ **4.** $16 = 16$

Problem Set D
1. $14 = 14$ **2.** $9 > 8$ **3.** $8 < 9$ **4.** $11 > 10$ **5.** $9 < 10$ **6.** $17 > 16$

Chapter 18. Grouping Numbers in 10s and 1s

1. three 10s, five 1s
2. seven 10s, six 1s
3. nine 10s, eight 1s
4. three 10s, one 1
5. four 10s, six 1s
6. 74
7. 55
8. 87
9. 17
10. 42

Chapter 19. Adding Three Numbers and Double- and Triple-Digit Numbers

Adding Three Numbers

1. 19	**2.** 12	**3.** 15	**4.** 19	**5.** 12	**6.** 14
7. 16	**8.** 17	**9.** 17	**10.** 19	**11.** 15	**12.** 19

Adding Double- and Triple-Digit Numbers

1. 69	**2.** 78	**3.** 69	**4.** 96	**5.** 84	**6.** 27
7. 87	**8.** 38	**9.** 79	**10.** 67	**11.** 88	**12.** 99
13. 259	**14.** 998	**15.** 889	**16.** 575	**17.** 986	**18.** 789
19. 999	**20.** 976	**21.** 858	**22.** 799	**23.** 885	**24.** 976

Chapter 20. Subtracting Single-, Double-, and Triple-Digit Numbers

Subtracting Single-Digit Numbers

1. 8	**2.** 5	**3.** 7	**4.** 4	**5.** 10	**6.** 3
7. 11	**8.** 5	**9.** 11	**10.** 9	**11.** 7	**12.** 10
13. 11	**14.** 7	**15.** 14	**16.** 7	**17.** 3	**18.** 9

Subtracting Double-Digit Numbers

1. 32	**2.** 60	**3.** 21	**4.** 15	**5.** 21	**6.** 12
7. 16	**8.** 17	**9.** 17	**10.** 24	**11.** 11	**12.** 20

Subtracting Triple-Digit Numbers

1. 214	**2.** 633	**3.** 212
4. 109	**5.** 220	**6.** 217
7. 241	**8.** 641	**9.** 747

Chapter 21. Word Problems in Addition and Subtraction

1. $9 + 6 = 15$
2. $3 + 4 + 5 = 12$
3. $4 + 7 + 3 = 14$
4. $8 + 5 + 6 = 19$
5. $5 + 7 = 12; 18 - 12 = 6$
6. $68 - 31 = 37$
7. $97 - 24 = 73$
8. $19 - 5 = 14; 14 - 4 = 10$

Chapter 22. Regrouping, Expanded Notation, and Graphing

Regrouping and Expanded Notation

1. $24 = 20 + 4$
   $\underline{+38 = 30 + 8}$
   $\quad\quad 50 + 12 = 62$

2. $53 = 50 + 3$
   $\underline{+29 = 20 + 9}$
   $\quad\quad 70 + 12 = 82$

3. $49 = 40 + 9$
   $\underline{+34 = 30 + 4}$
   $\quad\quad 70 + 13 = 83$

4. $67 = 60 + 7$
   $\underline{+18 = 10 + 8}$
   $\quad\quad 70 + 15 = 85$

Graphing 100s, 10s, and 1s

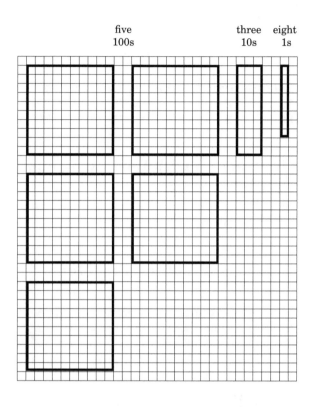

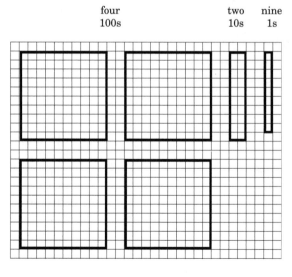

Chapter 23. Addition with Carrying

Adding Two Double-Digit Numbers with Carrying

1. 71	**2.** 53	**3.** 87	**4.** 75	**5.** 98	**6.** 83
7. 91	**8.** 72	**9.** 32	**10.** 70	**11.** 94	**12.** 68
13. 93	**14.** 64	**15.** 95	**16.** 91	**17.** 62	**18.** 84

Adding Three Double-Digit Numbers with Carrying

1. 52	**2.** 75	**3.** 91	**4.** 78	**5.** 74	**6.** 97
7. 82	**8.** 83	**9.** 61	**10.** 87	**11.** 81	**12.** 91

Chapter 24. Subtraction with Borrowing and Review of Carrying and Borrowing

1. 39	**2.** 24	**3.** 28	**4.** 24	**5.** 58	**6.** 75
7. 16	**8.** 19	**9.** 29	**10.** 25	**11.** 52	**12.** 48

Chapter 25. Adding and Subtracting Money

1. 80 cents − (10 + 5 cents) = 80 − 15 cents = 65 cents
2. 75 cents − (25 + 5 + 5 + 3 cents) = 75 − 38 cents = 37 cents
3. 94 cents − (25 + 10 + 4 cents) = 94 − 39 cents = 55 cents
4. 87 cents − (25 + 10 + 10 + 5 + 5 cents) = 87 − 55 cents = 32 cents
5. 92 cents − (25 + 25 + 5 + 5 + 5 + 6 cents) = 92 − 71 cents = 21 cents

Chapter 26. Word Problems in Addition and Subtraction

1.

$$\begin{array}{r} 7 \\ -5 \\ \hline 2 \text{ more} \end{array} \qquad \begin{array}{r} 7 \\ +5 \\ \hline 12 \end{array} \qquad \begin{array}{r} 29 \\ -12 \\ \hline 17 \text{ left} \end{array}$$

2.

$$\begin{array}{r} {}^{4\,1}\!\cancel{5}4 \\ -\ 6 \\ \hline 48 \end{array} \qquad \begin{array}{r} {}^{1} \\ 48 \\ +\ 4 \\ \hline 52 \text{ left} \end{array}$$

3.

$$\begin{array}{r} 10 \\ +7 \\ \hline 17 \text{ altogether} \end{array} \qquad \begin{array}{r} 10 \\ -\ 7 \\ \hline 3 \text{ more} \end{array}$$

4.

$$\begin{array}{r} {}^{1} \\ 5 \\ 4 \\ +7 \\ \hline 16 \text{ altogether} \end{array}$$

5.

$$\begin{array}{r} {}^{7\,1}\!\cancel{8}0 \\ -61 \\ \hline 19 \text{ left} \end{array}$$

6.

$$\begin{array}{r} {}^{8\,1}\!\cancel{9}4 \\ -55 \\ \hline 39 \text{ boys} \end{array}$$

Chapter 27. Telling Time

Telling Time on Conventional Clocks (Minilesson 71)

1. **a.** one twenty, or twenty after one
    b. eleven thirty-five, or twenty-five of twelve
    c. two forty, or twenty of three
    d. twelve forty-five, or a quarter of one

2.

Telling Time on Digital Clocks

3. **a.** four thirty-five, or twenty-five of five
    b. six forty-five, or a quarter of seven
    c. one fifty, or ten of two
    d. nine fifty-five, or five of ten

4. **a.**   3:10
    b.   1:55
    c.   12:40
    d.   5:50

Chapter 28. Advanced Counting

1. twenty-six
2. eighty-seven
3. fifty
4. thirty-six
5. 15, 25, 40, 50
6. 200, 202, 204
7. 50, 60, 75, 85
8. 866, 868, 871, 873

Chapter 29. Introduction to Multiplication and Division

Problem Set A
1. 24
2. 30
3. 70
4. 18
5. 32
6. 45

Problem Set B
1. 28
2. 27
3. 28
4. 27
5. 16
6. 30
7. 60
8. 40

Chapter 30. Shapes and Measurements

1. **a.** 12
   b. 36
2. 24 inches = 12 + 12 inches = 2 feet
3. 42 inches = 12 + 12 + 12 + 6 inches = 3 feet 6 inches
4. 2 yards = 36 + 36 inches = 72 inches
5. 3 yards = 3 + 3 + 3 feet = 9 feet
6. 15 feet = 3 + 3 + 3 + 3 + 3 feet = 5 yards
7. 30 inches = 12 + 12 + 6 inches = 2 feet 6 inches
8. 1 foot 4 inches = 12 + 4 inches = 16 inches
9. 1 yard 3 inches = 36 + 3 inches = 39 inches

Index